$12

J
973.7

The Battle of

GENERAL GEORGE H. THOMAS & THE MOST DE

Benson Bobrick

Alfred A. KNOPF New York

of Nashville

isive Battle of the Civil War

THIS IS A BORZOI BOOK PUBLISHED BY ALFRED A. KNOPF

Picture credits can be found on page 130.

Knopf, Borzoi Books, and the colophon are registered trademarks of Random House, Inc.

Visit us on the Web! www.randomhouse.com/kids

Educators and librarians, for a variety of teaching tools, visit us at www.randomhouse.com/teachers

Library of Congress Cataloging-in-Publication Data
Bobrick, Benson.
The Battle of Nashville / Benson Bobrick. — 1st ed.
p. cm.
ISBN 978-0-375-84887-2 (trade) — ISBN 978-0-375-94887-9 (lib. bdg.)
1. Nashville, Battle of, Nashville, Tenn., 1864—Juvenile literature.
2. Tennessee—History—Civil War, 1861–1865—Campaigns—Juvenile literature. I. Title.
E477.52.B63 2010
973.7'37—dc22
2009054072

The text of this book is set in 12.5-point Cochin.

MANUFACTURED IN CHINA
October 2010

10 9 8 7 6 5 4 3 2 1

First Edition

To Anthony Chiappelloni, Peter Guttmacher,
Robin Brownstein, and Peter Murkett,
fast friends and comrades all

—B.B.

ACKNOWLEDGMENTS

I had generous help in the making of this book, and would like to express my bountiful thanks to my splendid agent, Russell Galen; my wonderfully enthusiastic and dedicated editor, Michelle Frey; Carol Naughton, the production manager; Kate Gartner for her beautiful design; Rebecca Bullene for her superb selection of images and photographs; Karen Taschek for copyediting the text with such care; and Lisa Leventer, Janet Wygal, and Artie Bennett for diligent proofreading throughout. My wife, Hilary, gave of her love and support and (no mean critic) rightly pronounced the book a visual feast.

CONTENTS

That late autumn day, a gentle rain was falling. Not a breeze stirred the leafless branches of the trees. General Ulysses S. Grant stood in the doorway of his cabin and watched the raindrops in the pale light of evening. Each drop, it seemed, was like the life of a soldier. One drop after another. They were all alike and seemed to fall for nothing on the ground. He went in and lay down on his bed. His headquarters were spartan, his needs those of a simple man. "I had a physique that could stand anything," he would write. "Whether I slept on the ground or in a tent, whether I slept one hour or ten . . . made no difference. I could lie down and sleep in the rain without caring." At least now he had a roof over his head.

It was 1864. As general in chief of the Union armies, Grant ran the war from a log cabin on the banks of the James River at City Point, Virginia. In the American Civil War, the Union army was the Army of the North, and so called because most of those fighting against the South wanted to preserve the Union of all the states.

Grant's quarters had two rooms. There were an iron camp bedstead and washstand in one of them, and in the other a plain pine table and some wooden chairs. Nearby was a telegraph office, which constantly clicked with important messages that kept him up to date on every aspect of the war.

"Whether I slept on the ground or in a tent, whether I slept one hour or ten . . . made no difference. I could lie down and sleep in the rain without caring."

General Ulysses S. Grant stands in front of his campaign tent at his headquarters in Cold Harbor, Virginia, 1864.

Some of Grant's subordinate generals were making headway. At least, their armies were on the move. His own was going nowhere. It had been at City Point all summer, where he had hoped to have a victory over Robert E. Lee, head of the Army of Northern Virginia—the main Confederate army in the East. But Grant's army had stalled. So it was there that he would have to winter it out.

Grant was a slight, wiry man, five feet, seven inches tall and 150 pounds. He was stern, sullen at times, and given to long, awkward silences, even on social occasions. That tended to unnerve people who didn't know him well. Perhaps because of his solitary ways, he smoked like a chimney (about twenty cigars a day) and drank too much. President Lincoln didn't care, or judge him for that, so long as he won his battles and moved the war along. One day when someone complained to Lincoln about Grant's drinking, the president said: "Tell me the brand of his whiskey and I'll send it to my other generals, too."

There was a bond between the two men. Both had known hard times and had come up from relatively humble beginnings, though Lincoln had been poorer. Born to frontier drifters in backwoods Kentucky in a shack with one window and a door, Lincoln had grown up with almost no formal schooling and had learned to write with a piece of charcoal on a wooden shovel "scraped clean with a drawing knife." But he read a lot and, after a shiftless youth, finally got his bearings. Eventually he became a wealthy lawyer, a great and powerful politician, and an eloquent man.

At six feet, four inches, Lincoln towered above Grant, as he did above most men. Whereas Grant, though small, looked like any soldier, everything about Lincoln was unusual or strange. He had a scarecrow-like appearance, stoop-shouldered, with a ramshackle build, large, dark features, and rebellious hair. His wrinkled, weathered skin was rough as bark and his whole demeanor manly. Yet the backwoods twang of his voice was pitched almost as high as a girl's.

For all that, there was a dignity, compassion, and wisdom in him that won the nation's heart. Though an intellectual of sorts, he was a man of the people. He liked to talk to soldiers, and when he visited their camp and passed by the long rows of tents, he showed an interest in everything

that touched their daily lives. They could see by his kindly, sorrow-stricken face that he cared for them. His fatherly concern moved them deeply and they often called him Father Abraham.

When he happened upon them at mess, he would say, "That coffee smells good, boys. Give me a cup," or, "How are these beans, boys? Let me have a plate." But left to himself, he often ate little—some fruit, perhaps, with crackers and milk.

President Lincoln visits
General George B. McClellan
and his troops near Sharpsburg,
Maryland, on October 3, 1862,
a few weeks after the Battle of Antietam.

His dress was as plain as his food. At the White House, he sometimes received guests in his slippers or wore a faded coat a bit short at the sleeves. In winter, on going out, he sometimes wrapped himself in an old gray shawl instead of an overcoat.

Lincoln hated cruelty of any kind and at every chance tempered justice with mercy. He pardoned many a soldier condemned by military courts to be shot and once, after letting some draft resisters go, remarked: "Die when I may, I wish it said of me by those who knew me best that I always plucked a thistle and planted a flower where I thought a flower would grow." Nothing gave Lincoln keener satisfaction than to prevent an injustice or to lighten the burden of some suffering soul. When he wrote a telegram to prevent an execution, he was so anxious that it be sent on time that he often went in person to the telegraph office, as late as midnight, to send it himself.

Lincoln was witty, even funny at times, and a great storyteller. But there was a deep, tender sadness in him that marked his features as he aged. He had known for a long time that an assassin would one day take him. He believed in omens and found prophetic meaning in dreams. Once he dreamed that he saw two images of himself in a mirror. One image was full of life, vigor, energy, and strength; the other inert and lifeless, stretched straight out on a couch. Some people today might call him superstitious. He would just say that he knew that beyond our senses, there was a secret shape to things.

Grant considered himself too down-to-earth for that. Though he might have wondered. The unexpected had played a large role in his life. Unlike Lincoln, Grant had started out with an advantage or two. He had worked in a tannery and on a family-owned farm before attending West

This photograph of a young, beardless Abraham Lincoln was taken in 1855 when he ran for the U.S. Senate.

Point. He wasn't much of a student, though—he did poorly in a number of subjects, including military tactics, and stood near the bottom of an unusually weak class. But he excelled at horsemanship. When he rode a horse, a fellow cadet recalled, it was as if "man and beast were one."

On graduation he went off to fight in the Mexican War, serving with distinction. But after that he started on a downward career. He sought comfort in drink and had to resign from the army to escape court-martial on the charge of drunkenness. Poverty dogged his footsteps. He failed at every job he tried. By 1860, at age thirty-eight, he could barely make ends meet. On the eve of the Civil War he was selling firewood on a street corner in Galena, Illinois.

A newspaper vendor with his horse-drawn cart sells papers in Virginia with news of Grant's early victories, 1863.

The war gave him a second chance. Grant had a stomach for violence (some would say too much), and he was quick to volunteer. That is not to say he was not patriotic. But the one thing that gave him energy in life was war. Based on his prior service, he was made a colonel, but the soldiers in his unit gave him little respect at first. He looked untidy, even shabby, and wore a battered plug hat. One day a few of his soldiers jostled him on purpose and knocked his hat to the ground. He stooped and picked it up and brushed it off calmly. Then he turned and gave them such a hard, cold stare that chills went up their spines. They never crossed him again. In time, Grant proved an able soldier and rose through the ranks. He was as tenacious as a terrier. Some of his early victories were costly, but they made the headlines of the day. He had helped capture two important forts on the Tennessee and Cumberland rivers—Forts Henry and Donelson—led Union forces at the Battle of Shiloh (Tennessee) and in the Siege of Vicksburg on the Mississippi River, and was credited with the Union victory at Chattanooga, Tennessee. By 1864, he had become a household name. Lincoln, partly for political reasons, had chosen Grant to head his armies and thought he might turn out to be the great commander he had long been searching for.

That was now in doubt. Grant's great opponent in the East was Robert E. Lee. Grant had had a plan to beat him. Grant was to grind Lee's army down with overwhelming force. At the beginning of May, Grant had put this plan into motion. At the time, Lee's army was dug in behind the Rapidan River in Virginia. It was too strong to be attacked head-on. So Grant had to turn one of its flanks. Lee's left was protected by fieldworks—log and stone fencing, make-shift ramparts, and sharpened stakes—which reached to the spurs of the Blue Ridge Mountains. His right was protected by fortified trenches and a stream called Mine Run. Between the two armies stood a tract of land called the Wilderness. It was covered with a dense growth of pine, oak, chestnut, and hazel. It was the hardest kind of ground to deploy in or advance through under fire. Grant had about 120,000 men, Lee 73,000. But Lee knew the ground.

The contest began on May 5 as the two armies struck at

Civil War artist Edwin Forbes's 1862 drawing of General N. P. Banks's corps crossing the Blue Ridge Mountains through Chester Gap.

7

each other through the woods. The fighting became so fierce that in places the woods caught fire. Lee's right flank was broken, but Grant's right was also mauled. Neither army wanted to renew the battle. Grant had lost almost 20,000 men. Lee's losses were also heavy, and the South was running out of men, so unlike Grant's, they could not be replaced. That was the grim equation on which Grant now relied. He advanced. The two armies clashed again at Spotsylvania Courthouse. Once more the Union casualties were awful. Still, Grant came on. Cold Harbor followed, where Grant had to carve his rifle pits in a marsh. Even before the fighting, his men died in scores from malaria, a mosquito-borne disease. Then, in his first blind assault, he lost more than 7,000 men in half an hour. Next, he worked his way around south of Richmond to Petersburg, Virginia, crossed the James River, and began a long siege of the town. That left Washington, D.C., unprotected, and a Rebel general swept through the Shenandoah Valley to its outskirts, filling the city with alarm.

Well before that, Lincoln decided he had better pay a surprise visit to Grant's quarters. He arrived by river steamer, accompanied only by his young son Tad. In the offhand manner he sometimes adopted, he told Grant, "I just thought I would jump aboard a boat and come down. I don't expect I can do any good." But he looked all business. This time, he was dressed in a formal black suit and wore his famous tall black stovepipe hat. "He looked like an undertaker," one of Grant's aides said. Lincoln wanted to talk about the progress of the war. He took off his hat and set it down gently on the split-pine table. Then he ran his rawboned fingers through his hair. He fixed his eyes on Grant and asked him what was going on.

Far to the west, Brigadier General George H. Thomas of the Army of the North sat twisting his beard into braided strands as he looked out across the bluffs above the Cumberland River. He worked at his beard this way whenever he was lost in thought. Recently, he had turned the city of Nashville, Tennessee, into a fortress. But the enemy was fast approaching, and he still had much to do. He had raw troops to train, civilians to arm, trenches and rifle pits to dig. Above all, he needed cavalry horses—8,000 to 10,000 more than he had. Where in the world could he find them? Yet cavalry was the key to his whole battle plan. He was thinking about this, and other challenges besides.

Of late, the War Department in Washington had been hounding him with foolish telegrams. These urged him to take actions that would have damaged his army. For example, they urged him to attack before he was ready—before all his men were in place, or rightly trained, or fully armed. He wasn't about to do that. He was too good a general to give in to unwise pressure and too decent a man to risk the welfare of his men. Yet each time he received a telegram, he had to take time out of his day to answer it. Some of the telegrams came from Henry Halleck, known as Old Brains, Lincoln's army chief of staff; others came from Edwin M. Stanton, Lincoln's secretary of war. Halleck was a military intellectual and "armchair soldier" who seemed to know little about the practical aspects of war. Stanton was an able man, but hot-tempered and impatient—the sort of person who always has a red face. And then there were the strange telegrams from Grant, who tried to second-guess everything Thomas did. After some weeks of this interference, Thomas's patience was wearing thin. He frowned upon the motives behind the interference. Halleck and Stanton, he thought, were just misled. But Grant was jealous and

General George H. Thomas,
circa 1860s.

malicious. He had been nursing a grudge against Thomas for a long time. Ever since Thomas had been promoted over him (after the Battle of Shiloh, where Grant had been caught off guard), Grant had viewed Thomas as a powerful rival. He also knew Thomas didn't think much of him as a general. Well, that was too bad. Thomas breathed deeply and sighed. Then he let it go. He had too much to do. But as he gave his beard one last, coiled twist, he also marveled at the strange sequence of events that had placed the fate of the nation in his hands.

This is the story of the single most important battle of the American Civil War. For four long years, the armies of the North and South had opposed each other in bloody conflict. Almost half a million men had been killed. Whole regions had been ruined or laid waste. In the great battles of Gettysburg, Antietam, Shiloh, Chancellorsville, and Chickamauga, the two sides had battered each other senseless. The North had made gains, but could do nothing decisive. That would change completely with the Battle of Nashville, in December 1864.

CHAPTER TWO

WHY THE CIVIL WAR WAS FOUGHT

It has been said that Americans will never forget the Civil War for the same reason that people never forget when their house burns down. That's what happened when the war took place—America's house was engulfed in flames. No one could have foreseen the length of the conflict or the unspeakable scale of its violence. More than half a million men were killed. In the end, almost as many Americans perished in the Civil War as in all of the nation's other wars combined.

What had brought about this horrible calamity? Up until the fighting began, America had seemed a young, vibrant, and thriving nation. In the seventy-odd years since it had won its independence from Great Britain, the number of its states had more than doubled, from thirteen to thirty-four, and waves of immigration had caused the population to grow at a stunning pace. American settlers had crossed the Allegheny Mountains, streamed into the Mississippi Valley, and pushed on to the Pacific coast. Canals, railroads, and navigable waterways bound North, South,

East, and West together. Agriculture flourished in the South and Midwest. Industry boomed in the North. The mineral resources of the country, like coal and iron, were being mined at a terrific rate. The romance of the Wild West had also taken hold. In the West, pioneers and other settlers kept spreading out and moving across deserts and mountains and into the Great Plains. There was a ragged edge of roving and lawless adventure to it, and many people were ruined in the hectic pace of the nation's westward march. But Americans seemed able to overcome all obstacles that stood in their path.

Yet all the while a fatal disease had been eating away at the country's heart.

That disease was slavery.

In America, from colonial times on, black people had been owned by whites. In the Declaration of Independence, Thomas Jefferson had said: "We hold these truths to be self-evident, that all men are created equal, that they are endowed by their Creator with certain unalienable Rights, that among these are Life, Liberty and the pursuit of Happiness." But slaves had not been covered by that noble pronouncement. Not only did they lack freedom, but a clause in the Constitution counted each one as "three-fifths" of a man.

In effect, they had been left out of the American dream.

Between the sixteenth and nineteenth centuries, approximately 650,000 black Africans had been abducted from their homelands and brought to the United States. Many had been shipped across the Atlantic Ocean with the complicity of New England rum merchants and traders. But by the 1800s, the slave trade had languished and slavery was illegal in the North. Most slaves in America by then had been born into their abject state. Yet slavery, centered in the South, dominated American life. It cast its long shadow over national politics, local and congressional debate, and all the issues of territorial expansion within the United States.

Though slavery was justified by its defenders for social and economic reasons—for example, it was said to make up for the scarcity of free labor in a rural economy in which every free man could occupy land if he chose—it had no moral basis. Its sole source was the desire of Europeans in a languid climate to have the work done for them instead of doing it themselves.

The interior view of a slave pen, showing the doors of cells where the slaves were held before being sold, Alexandria, Virginia, circa early 1860s.

Some blacks worked as household servants; others toiled in the fields. On the cotton plantations especially, they worked under the lash like beasts of burden. They lived in hovels. The clothes they wore were rags. During harvest and milling time, they worked up to sixteen hours a day. Sometimes women had to help with the plowing and hoeing, which in those days was usually considered "men's work." Even little

George N. Barnard, official photographer of the Chief Engineer's Office, took this photo of a slave auction house on Whitehall Street in Atlanta, Georgia, in 1864.

children worked as water carriers and at other chores. Some slaves were treated better than others. But bondage is bondage. Under the law, blacks had no rights that whites had to respect. Slaves were property. Fugitive slaves were hunted down like wild beasts.

Such a system could only corrupt the feelings of those who condoned it or relied on it for the wealth, comforts, and leisure they enjoyed. The idea that one human being must serve all the needs and appetites of another is inherently undignified. The whole culture of slavery was also so different from the independent world of the Western farmer and the free-enterprise bustle of the North that two different nations had grown up within the United States.

The lead-up to the final break was complex. The South had plenty of friends in the North, including powerful banking and commercial interests that depended on cotton, the main slave commodity of the South. There were also a number of Western farmers of Southern descent. At the same time, though Northerners might have accepted slavery in the South, the expansion of slavery into the unoccupied West, which was regarded by both Northern farmers and new immigrants as a "promised land," was another matter. The West was supposed to be the land of equal opportunity—a land where small as well as large farms could flourish. But a slave-based plantation economy kept down not only blacks but also poorer whites. Moreover, in such an economy poor whites lacked the means to contribute to local industrial development—unlike the salaried workers of the North. Slavery led to the rapid concentration of land and wealth and prevented the expansion of local commerce. Instead of providing a basis for industrial growth, the Southern countryside, economically dominated by a few large estates, provided only a limited market for industry. Yet instead of investing their own wealth in local industry, large plant-ers spent much of their money on luxuries obtained from overseas. That was not a good formula for healthy economic growth in the West.

North and South drifted further and further apart. In the early 1800s, the chief field of conflict between them was the new land in the West that had begun to open up. Was it to be slave? Or free? Political power hung in the balance, because according to the American system of proportional representation, the number of seats in Congress would in-crease for either side. Although in the Senate each state, regardless of the size of its population, had two senators, in the House of Representatives, more populous states had

"Map Showing the Comparitive [sic] *Area of the Northern and Southern States, East of the Rocky Mountains," from* Harper's Weekly, *February 23, 1861.*

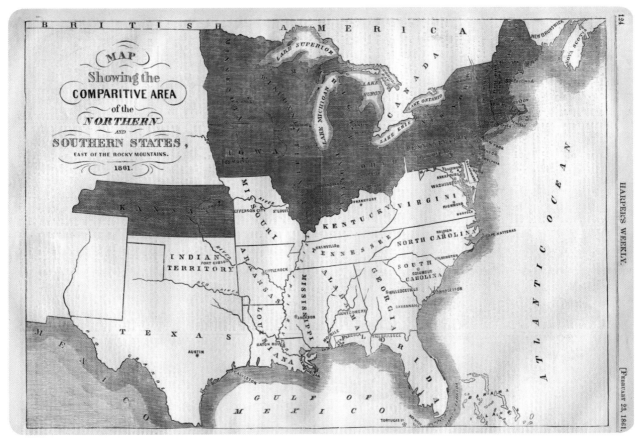

more representatives, in proportion to the size of the state's population. Also, since 1789, free and slave states had been admitted in pairs to ensure a balance, at least in the Senate. To be admitted as a state, a newly organized territory had to have a duly elected legislature and a state constitution that met the approval of the Congress of the United States. But in 1817, Missouri's demand to be admitted as a slave state had threatened to tip the scales. A compromise was reached in 1820 that barred the spread of slavery into the Northwest but allowed Missouri to come in as a slave state in conjunction with the free state of Maine.

The Missouri Compromise, as it was called, appeared to save the day. But as the years passed, the population of the free states increased faster than that of the slave states, giving them a numerical advantage in Congress. The South grew restless, and tempers flared.

As the new lands were occupied, settled, and formed into states, efforts were made at a new compromise. In Congress, those in favor of slavery and those opposed to it clashed. The debates were heated, even violent. On one occasion—in May 1856—a Southern congressman, Preston Brooks of South Carolina, beat senseless a Northern senator, Charles Sumner of Massachusetts, with his cane. Sumner had called for repeal of the Fugitive Slave Law, which obliged Northerners to return escaped slaves to their place of bondage. He had also spoken out fiercely against the spread of slavery. Brooks came up to him as he was writing at his desk in the Senate and attacked him without warning while a fellow Southerner stood by with his pistol drawn to prevent anyone from intervening. The cane broke before Brooks would stop, and it took three years for Sumner to recover from his wounds.

Some in the North, known as Abolitionists, wanted to abolish the whole institution of slavery. They felt that it was

ARGUMENTS OF THE CHIVALRY.

A dramatic portrayal, published in the Northern press on May 22, 1856, of the attack on Massachusetts senator Charles Sumner by Representative Preston S. Brooks of South Carolina.

immoral, evil, and degrading. Others hoped only to prevent its spread. They believed they could not do away with slavery directly because it was legal. But they also believed it could not sustain itself as the rest of the nation grew. The awkward truth is, the Constitution of the United States allowed for slavery (until the Constitution was amended after the war). It was therefore legal in the states where it existed. But a national majority became convinced that slavery would eventually wither and die of its own accord if it could be restricted to where it already was.

One crisis followed another. Then, in 1850, a quarrel arose over the status of California. This was resolved in a compromise that admitted California into the Union as a free state and banned the slave trade in the District of Columbia but left open the fate of New Mexico and Utah. It also made the Fugitive Slave Law harsher than before. But that failed to ease tensions. By 1850, one senator, John Sherman of Ohio, could say: "There is really no Union now between the North and the South. . . . No two nations upon

An 1844 illustrated sheet music cover for an Abolitionist song composed by Jesse Hutchinson, Jr.

"GET OFF THE TRACK!"

A song for Emancipation, sung by
THE HUTCHINSONS,
Respectfully Dedicated to
NATH P. ROGERS,

JESSE HUTCHINSON JUN.

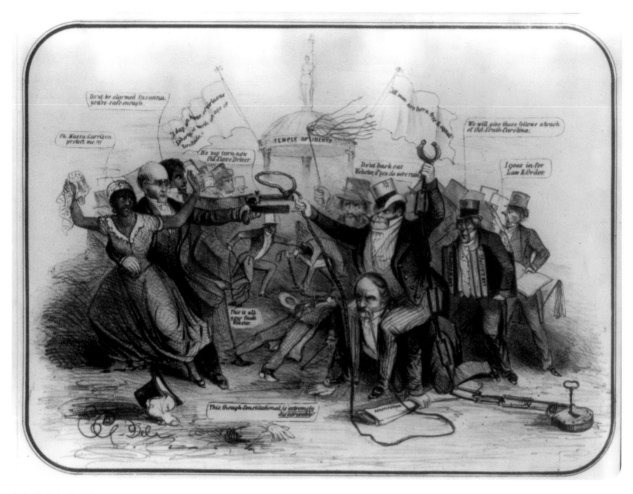

A cartoon satirizing the antagonism between Northern Abolitionists and supporters of the Fugitive Slave Act of 1850.

earth entertain feelings of more bitter rancor toward each other than these two sections of the Republic."

Two events helped bring the issue to a head. One was the repeal of the Missouri Compromise of 1820 (which had prohibited the extension of slavery) by the Kansas-Nebraska Act of 1854 (which allowed it to spread). The second was the Dred Scott decision of the Supreme Court in 1857. The case had been brought by Dred Scott, a slave in Missouri who had formerly lived in the free state of Illinois. He appealed to the Court for the restitution of his freedom. But the Court declared that a black person was not a citizen and had no rights that the white man was bound to respect, and that slave owners could hold slaves as property in the North as well as the South. That meant that slavery could even be reintroduced into states where it had been abolished, as well as into any new state that might be formed.

Abolitionists were defiant. They rejected the decision of the Court and flouted the Fugitive Slave Law. An "underground railroad"—a large, loose network of sympathetic people with safe houses—was organized to help fugitive slaves escape to the Northern states and to Canada, where they were safe under the British flag. A few Northern states even passed Liberty Bills, giving slaves full rights. Meanwhile, Harriet Beecher Stowe's *Uncle Tom's Cabin*, a book that portrayed the sad plight of slaves, took Europe as well as America by storm.

The South boiled with fury.

Madness was in the air. On October 16, 1859, the white Abolitionist John Brown, crazed by the recent murder of his son, attacked Harpers Ferry, at the mouth of the Shenandoah Valley, and with a small armed band captured the Federal armory and arsenal, seized the bridge across the Potomac, cut the telegraph wires, and took possession of the town. His scheme was to establish a stronghold in the mountains of Virginia and, by raising a slave revolt, establish an army of liberated slaves that would sweep through

An 1899 photograph of Abolitionist John Brown.

the South. His plot failed completely, and he was captured and hanged. But many in the North viewed him as a martyr. Even today, we remember his exploits in "John Brown's Body," the stirring soldiers' song. Its famous refrain, "His soul goes marching on," was fervently sung by Northern troops in camp and on the march throughout the war.

The turbulent times gave birth to new political parties, such as the Free Soil Party (which wanted to prevent the spread of slavery) and the Know-Nothing Party, which hoped to suppress the new immigrant vote. Another long-standing party, the Whig Party, died out. The Republican Party was also born, built on a platform that included abolishing slavery. When the new Republican Party was organized, it drew in nearly all those opposed to slavery, North and South. Abraham Lincoln joined the party when it was first organized in 1856 in Illinois. All his life he had believed that slavery was wrong, because he believed no man had a right to own another. Two years later, he ran for the United States Senate against Stephen A. Douglas, who had sponsored the Kansas-Nebraska Act.

Lincoln saw that a nation could not contain two com-

This 1859 engraving shows hostage taking and bloodshed inside the engine house of the Harpers Ferry Armory, which John Brown and his cohorts had seized.

pletely separate societies. He saw also that it was slavery that made them different. In a famous speech, he declared, "A house divided against itself cannot stand. I believe this government cannot endure, permanently, half slave and half free. I do not expect the Union to be dissolved; I do not expect the house to fall; but I do expect it will cease to be divided. It will become all one thing, or all the other."

When he showed this speech in advance to some friends, only one of them, William Herndon, his law partner, thought it was good. The others thought his opinions were too strong. They were afraid he would be branded an extremist. But Lincoln was convinced the crisis facing the country had to be framed in stark, dramatic terms. He told them: "Friends, this thing has been delayed long enough. The time has come when these sentiments should be uttered, and if it is decreed that I should go down because of this speech, then let me go down linked with the truth—let me die in the advocacy of what is just and right."

Lincoln and Douglas faced off in a series of seven debates held across the state of Illinois. It was a close contest, and Douglas won the election by a narrow margin. But the campaign made Lincoln a figure of national renown. Two years later, in 1860, he ran as the Republican candidate for president of the United States. In some ways, Lincoln seemed the ideal person to bridge the national divide. After all, although a man of the North, he had a Southern wife,

> "A house divided against itself cannot stand. I believe this government cannot endure, permanently, half slave and half free. . . ."

This 1860 political cartoon shows rival presidential nominees Lincoln and Douglas matched in a footrace, with Lincoln pulling ahead thanks to his long strides. The U.S. Capitol is shown on the right.

Southern ancestry, and a disposition inclined toward compromise. But after he was nominated, all hope of healing the bitter wounds between North and South seemed to fade.

For forty years, the nation had been sitting on a powder keg. Lincoln's victory in November 1860 lit the fuse. Southerners were unwilling to live under an administration that they viewed as hostile to their whole way of life. They had threatened before the election to break away if he won. Now they carried through with that threat. South Carolina took the lead and seceded—that is, separated from the Union—on December 20, 1860, even before Lincoln could be sworn in as president of the United States. By February 1, 1861, six other states of the Deep South (Alabama, Florida, Georgia, Louisiana, Mississippi, and Texas) had followed suit. In each case, secession was authorized by the state legislature, which insisted its act of separation was lawful under the Constitution. At the same time, the breakaway states declared themselves no longer bound by the Constitution and laws of the United States. They also took possession of public property within their borders, such as mints (which printed money), arsenals, and forts. In February 1861, their representatives organized a provisional government and Jefferson Davis was chosen president of the Confederate States of America. In one of his first pronouncements, Davis said: "All we ask is to be left alone." That was hardly possible. In Lincoln's view, the whole future of democratic government was at stake because the breakaway states had defied the principle of majority rule.

Meanwhile, Congress panicked, and in a series of desperate measures gave the South almost everything they sought—including legislation that would have enshrined slavery forever in the law. Such a resolution actually passed the House and Senate by wide margins. But it never became law because Lincoln refused to sign the bill.

At the same time, Lincoln was keenly aware that in the border states of Maryland, Kentucky, and Missouri, there were many pro-slavery people who were also pro-Union. It was imperative that those states not cast their lot with the South. "These all against us," he said, "and the job on our hands is too large for us. We might as well consent to separation at once, including the surrender of the capital"—the seat of the national government itself, in Washington, D.C.

An 1861 photograph of the
inauguration of Abraham Lincoln.
The dome of the U.S. Capitol was under
construction at the time.

In an atmosphere of crisis, Lincoln made his way to the capital, entered it by night, and on March 4 was inaugurated under military guard. In his inaugural address, he promised to do everything in his power to preserve the Union and pledged to maintain the authority of the Federal government with respect to its own property in every state. At the same time, he promised to do this without "bloodshed or violence," unless these were forced upon him by the South. "In *your* hands, my dissatisfied fellow-countrymen, and not in *mine*," he said, "is the momentous issue of civil war. The Government will not assail *you*. You can have no conflict without being yourselves the aggressors. *You* have no oath registered in Heaven to destroy the Government, while I shall have the most solemn one to 'preserve, protect, and defend it.'"

Not everyone in the South wanted to break away. During the election, there had been four candidates representing four parties. A majority of votes in the South were actually cast for those who wanted the Union preserved. But the landowning aristocracy of the South favored secession, and even welcomed a confrontation with the North to bring the whole issue of slavery to a head. Its members held most of the important positions in the state governments—in short, the reins of power.

All eyes now turned to Fort Sumter, in the harbor of Charleston, South Carolina, which was garrisoned by a handful of Federal, or Union, troops. Most of the forts, arsenals, post offices, harbor installations, and other Federal property in the breakaway states had already been seized by those in rebellion. But Fort Sumter had not. It soon became a test case for whether the South would actually attack Federal troops and whether those troops would defend their ground. By March, the garrison was running out of food and other supplies. When Lincoln tried to send some in, the Confederates opened fire. The shelling continued without ceasing for thirty-four hours, until the fort was ablaze. The fort fired back, but the Confederate harbor installations were much stronger and had more formidable guns. They were also protected by sloping iron plates slicked with grease. When the cannonballs from the fort struck them, they bounced off like India-rubber balls.

The citizens of Charleston rejoiced. They gathered on their rooftops to witness the action. Even ladies in expensive gowns went down to the wharves. At noon on April 14, the fort surrendered and the Stars and Stripes came down.

Until then, the people of the North had been reluctant to take up arms. But now they were willing, even eager, to fight. In that sense, Fort Sumter was the Bunker Hill of the Civil War. In the American Revolution, the Battle of Bunker Hill, in Boston, had rallied the colonists against the British. The colonists lost that battle but could say afterward that the British had started the war. That's what happened now. Northern feeling against secession surged. The next day, April 15, Lincoln declared the seceded states in rebellion and issued a call for 75,000 three-month volunteers. The volunteers poured in, but the price of Lincoln's call to arms was high, as four more states—Virginia, Arkansas, Tennessee, and North Carolina—joined the revolt.

And so the Civil War began. At the outset, it was not fought to abolish slavery, as many people today imagine, but to preserve the Union and its binding principle of majority rule. As Lincoln told Horace Greeley,

the editor of the *New York Tribune*, "My paramount object in this struggle is to save the Union, and it is not either to save or destroy slavery. If I could save the Union without freeing any slave I would do it, and if I could do it by freeing all the slaves I would do it; and if I could do it by freeing some and leaving others alone, I would also do that."

A painting of Fort Sumter.

The war took place in two general regions, or on two main fronts—the East, extending from the Atlantic Ocean to the Appalachian Mountains; and the West, from the Appalachian Mountains to the Mississippi River and beyond. In the East, the main objective of the North was to capture the Confederate capital of Richmond, Virginia. The main objective in the

An illustration of the Union troop recruitment centers in New York City.

West was to seize control of the Mississippi River and cut the Confederacy in two.

Lincoln had almost no experience of war. As a young congressman, he had opposed the Mexican War as a war of aggression, and when someone once asked him if he remembered anything about the War of 1812, which took place when he was a child, he recalled, "I had been fishing one day and caught a little fish, which I was taking home. I met a soldier in the road, and, having always been told at home that we must be good to the soldiers, I gave him my fish." Beyond that, at the age of twenty-three he had shouldered a rifle as the elected captain of a volunteer company during the Black Hawk War—a short conflict with an Indian chief. Lincoln himself saw no fighting. But he did save the life of an Indian from some enraged white men.

> "My paramount object in this struggle is to save the Union, and it is not either to save or destroy slavery. If I could save the Union without freeing any slave I would do it, and if I could do it by freeing all the slaves I would do it; and if I could do it by freeing some and leaving others alone, I would also do that."

Jefferson Davis, president of the newly formed Confederate States, on the other hand, had served as secretary of war under President Franklin Pierce. He knew all about warfare and the proper structure of an army. He knew about infantry, cavalry, and artillery units, and everything that went into their equipment and supply. Even before Lincoln's election, Davis had formed some elite fighting units and had been secretly accumulating arms. Many of the higher officers in the U.S. Army were also known to him personally, and so among those who chose the South, he knew at once whom to appoint to high commands. All this helped the South to organize itself more quickly for the fight ahead.

Yet at the beginning of the war, the North seemed to have the advantage: after all, twenty-three states (out of a total of thirty-four) had remained in the Union, including the border states of Maryland, Kentucky, and Missouri, as Lincoln had hoped. The western counties of Virginia (later West Virginia) also formed their own pro-Union state.

Moreover, the North was much more industrialized. It had five times as many manufacturing plants. It also had more people—about 22 million as compared to 9 million (including 4 million slaves) in the South. So the North had a huge manpower advantage. But it would need that to win. After all, it had to conquer the South. The South consisted of just eleven states, but together these made up a vast territory, twice as large as Portugal, France, and the British Isles combined. Also, the South didn't have to conquer the North or win in a military sense. It only had to hold out long enough for the will of the North to fail.

The truth is, the Federal government at the outset had almost no military power with which to enforce its will. The entire U.S. Army at the time consisted of 16,000 men, and most of these were on frontier duty in the West. That is, most were stationed at desert, river, and other outposts in newly formed territories along the Indian frontier. The

Jefferson Davis, president of the Confederate States of America, circa 1860.

entire U.S. Navy consisted of ninety ships, and only forty-two of these were in active service. That was hardly enough to patrol the Confederate coastline, which contained hundreds of inlets, bays, and river openings and stretched for a thousand miles from the Chesapeake Bay to the Gulf of Mexico. Even so, knowing that the South, with its lack of industry, would be strapped for war materiel, Lincoln proclaimed a naval blockade to prevent the South from getting arms and supplies from abroad.

An effective blockade was essential. Lincoln's great secretary of the navy, Gideon Welles, worked nonstop to build the navy up. He called it the military's "web feet." Over time, ships were repaired and new ones constructed. Some steamboats were converted into warships by means of steel plating and deck guns. One new type of gunboat was the steel ram, a little ship with great speed and a heavy prow, which was used to sink another ship by poking a hole in its side. Eventually, the navy had 671 ships or vessels to make its blockade work.

For their part, the Confederates hoped the blockade would backfire by provoking the hostility of European states. A number of those states, including Great Britain and France, depended on Southern products like cotton for their own industry and trade. They also depended on Southern markets for their goods. Throughout the war, a skillful corps of Northern diplomats persuaded France and Britain not to intervene in the conflict directly, though both powers gave the South some covert aid. Meanwhile, the South sought to make the naval blockade ineffective and engaged pirates and smugglers to obtain needed goods. They also developed fast blockade-running ships and invented the first underwater mine and torpedo boat. This torpedo boat (or tactical submarine) was a small, cigar-shaped vessel, propelled by

An 1863 engraving in Harper's Weekly *showing the wreck of the ironclad USS* Monitor *off Cape Hatteras, North Carolina.*

steam with a torpedo projecting from the bow. Finally, in the escalating contest, both sides constructed the first ironclad ships, which were covered with armor plate made from iron rails. In an epic battle at Hampton Roads, Virginia, the Confederate ironclad *Merrimack* and the Union *Monitor* fought each other to a draw.

That mutually destructive, even contest would eventually come to represent the seemingly endless stalemate of the war.

CHAPTER FOUR

GENERAL GEORGE H. THOMAS

Although the Civil War was a conflict between different regions, some communities and families were divided. Individuals, too, were torn. Robert E. Lee of Virginia, the greatest general of the South, thought slavery was evil. But he felt, after Virginia joined the Confederacy, that he could not raise his hand against his native state. Like many Southerners, he thought of his state as his country, to which his utmost patriotic allegiance was owed. General George H. Thomas, also of Virginia and the greatest general of the North, understood that the two—state and country—were not the same. He may have wavered briefly. But once he made up his mind, he never looked back. His wife recalled: "Whichever way he turned the matter over in his mind, his oath of allegiance to his government always came uppermost."

But his service in the war was caught between two worlds. The South condemned him because he fought for the North. The North didn't entirely trust him because his roots were in the South. For that reason,

unlike Ulysses S. Grant and William Tecumseh Sherman, for example, he had no one in Washington to promote his career. As a result, he didn't always receive the recognition he deserved. Meanwhile, his family never forgave him for making the choice he did. His sisters disowned him and in their home in Virginia turned his picture to the wall.

Yet there was something inevitable about the course he took. Even as a child, Thomas had been unusually idealistic. Though he was born in 1816 on a farm in Virginia worked by slaves, prejudice was foreign to his soul. Some of his playmates were black, and he would sometimes sneak treats to them and go off with them to look for raccoons and possums in the woods. "He loved the Negro quarters more than he did the great house," a friend said later, and he often played with the slave children under the great spreading oak tree in the yard. As soon as he was old enough to go to school, he also gave them Bible lessons and secretly taught them how to read and write. At night he would teach them what he learned at school each day, and he did all this "against his parents' orders." That was unheard of in Virginia at the time.

Southampton County, where Thomas was raised, was a remote sort of place, with dense forests and rolling hills dotted by farms, plantations, and "crossroad villages carved out of the woods." Around his house could be found a typical menagerie of dogs, chickens, hogs, cows, mules, and horses, with an apple orchard nearby and a brandy still out back. The district capital, or county seat, was a town called Jerusalem (in those days many places had biblical names), which consisted of little more than "a smoky cluster of buildings where pigs rooted in the street and old-timers spat tobacco in the shade." The area was also seamed with winding rivers and known for its bogs and swamps. The bogs, composed entirely of decayed vegetable fiber, swayed and shook underfoot. They had quaint names, like the Little Dismal, Alligator, Catfish, and Green. But they were dangerous places to go. Outlaws hid in them, and they were haunts for wild animals like wildcats and bears. Even so, young Thomas did his share of exploring when not under his parents' eye.

Thomas was not only a good-hearted child, he also had a lively mind. He took an interest in almost everything around him, including fine carpentry, saddle-making, and other crafts. When he learned something, he never forgot it. In later years, some would say there seemed to be nothing he didn't know. Yet he wasn't conceited in the least. In fact, he was so modest that if anybody praised him, he was apt to blush and lower his eyes. That would be true of him his whole life long. Though he would later stand firm and unshaken in every battle he ever fought in, with bullets flying all around, he trembled just once—when he received a standing ovation from Congress. That was the only time his hand was seen to shake.

General George H. Thomas,
date unknown.

When Thomas was twelve, his father died in a farm accident. That greatly increased his responsibilities at home. The family farm had some fifteen to twenty slaves, and Thomas now had to help supervise the plowing and planting, cut wood for fencing, and hollow out large sections of tree trunks for storage casks. Always he had to be on the lookout for raccoons, polecats, possums, and other predators that menaced what the farm produced. Though Thomas had an exceptionally good relationship with the slaves his family owned, when he was fifteen, he was almost killed in a local slave revolt. It so happened that a slave named Nat Turner, who worked on a neighboring farm, persuaded a number of

A drawing of Thomas's childhood home in Virginia.

28537 Chickamauga Drive

other slaves to rise up. Together, they formed a small but formidable military band that threatened the county even beyond the area in which Thomas lived.

The whole episode—the most famous slave uprising in American history—was tragic. All his life, Nat Turner had been a brave, gifted, eloquent, and upright man. He had been sold and resold as a slave, even though he had been led to believe as a boy that he might be freed. As the years passed and he grew older, he clung to a keen sense of his own self-worth. In the end, cruelty, frustration, and abuse pushed him over the edge.

In some ways, Turner was a lot like an Old Testament

A photograph of the one-room schoolhouse behind Thomas's childhood home.

prophet. He had heavenly visions that seemed divinely inspired. While working one day in the fields, he discovered "drops of dew like blood on the corn." In the woods, he found "leaves with strange characters and numbers etched on them. Other leaves contained the forms of men, like the figures in the sky." The Holy Spirit told him: "For as the blood of Christ had been shed on this earth, and had ascended to heaven for the salvation of sinners, and was now returning to earth again in the form of dew— and as the leaves on the trees bore the impression of the figures I had seen in the heavens, it was plain to me that the Savior was about to lay down the yoke he had borne

HORRID MASSACRE IN VIRGINIA.

An illustration of Nat Turner's Rebellion, 1831. This rebellion, led by an oppressed slave, was the largest slave uprising in American history.

for the sins of men, and the great day of Judgment was at hand."

He waited for a heavenly sign to launch his revolt. An eclipse of the sun seemed to provide it. He looked for another. On August 13, 1831, a second sign appeared. The sun dimmed and grew so pale it could be looked at directly. Then, changing hues, it went from green to blue to white. Finally, a black spot appeared on the sun's surface "like a black hand." At a meeting one night soon after in a clearing in the woods, Turner and his band drew a map of their campaigns with berry juice. The next day, they began to rampage through the county, killing as many whites as they could. Other slaves joined them, and their numbers increased from house to house. At each homestead, they armed themselves with more weapons—muskets, axes, and scythes. When the band approached the Thomas family farm, young George jumped into a wagon and fled for safety with his sisters and widowed mother into a nearby swamp. Apparently, their own slaves helped them get away.

Turner and his band passed on to other farms in a whirlwind, and before it was over, some 260 people lost their lives. Most of those who died were actually black and were killed at random by whites enraged by Turner's revolt. Turner himself escaped capture for many weeks, hiding out in the woods. "Alone with the fox's bark, the rabbit's rustle, and the screech-owl's scream," he dug a cave under some fence rails and—like Robinson Crusoe, marooned on his desert island—notched a stick to mark the days. Finally, he was discovered, brought to the county seat, tried, and hanged. But before his execution, he dictated his *Confessions,* which was a vivid and remarkable account of his life.

Most Southerners reacted to the revolt by demanding that laws against slaves be made even tougher than they were. But young George Thomas came to a different conclusion—that the desire for freedom in the human soul was too powerful to suppress.

Not long after the revolt, Thomas served for a brief time as a law clerk. Then, under the sponsorship of his local congressman, he went off to the United States Military Academy at West Point, in New York, to learn to be a soldier. At West Point, he lived in spartan simplicity in a sparsely

West Point cadets in a class photograph, 1865. Then, as now, West Point was the premier military academy in the United States. Most of the officers who served on both sides of the Civil War were West Point graduates.

furnished room. He shared the room with two other cadets — one of whom was William Tecumseh Sherman, who would also become a famous general. The room was hot in summer, cold in winter, poorly ventilated, and small. There was no running water — the cadets had to carry water to their rooms in buckets from an old-fashioned well worked with a pump.

Like all first-year cadets (or plebes), they were picked on by upperclassmen. But even then Thomas was fearless. When an upperclassman tried to bully him, Thomas threatened to throw him out the window. No one bothered him again. Of course, he got into some trouble himself now and then by breaking minor rules (such as horsing around after lights were out). But he was a solid student. In his four years at West Point, he learned about strategy and tactics, military engineering, the art of mechanical drawing, the science of ballistics, and other subjects useful to a captain of men.

Upon his graduation, Thomas joined an expedition in Florida against the Seminole Indians and proved his skill and courage in guerrilla warfare in the Everglades. Then he was sent to fight in the Mexican War. In several major battles, he was at the forefront of the action and received three promotions for bravery and skill. After the war, Thomas returned to West Point to teach. There he met and married a handsome woman named Frances Kellogg, who was spending the summer at a nearby hotel. By all accounts, the marriage was a happy one, of mutual love and respect. In the following year, he was sent to Fort Yuma (a desert fort, where the temperature was sometimes 100 degrees in the shade) before taking a post in Texas on the Indian frontier. It was dangerous service, since the Indians were understandably dissatisfied with their general treatment and the territories to which they were confined. While on patrol at Clear Fork along the Brazos River, Thomas tangled with some Comanches and was struck by an arrow in the chest. He promptly pulled it out and went on fighting. But the wound left an angry-looking wedge-shaped scar. Strangely enough, though he would later take part in many battles, this was the only wound he ever received.

During his frontier service, Thomas made good use of his time. Many officers gambled or drank just to make the days go by. Thomas was different. He studied animals and plants and the language of the local Indians. He even discovered a new kind of bat and compiled a dictionary of the dialect of the Yumas, one of the local Indian tribes. In Texas, he sat as a judge in several court-martial trials—along with Robert E. Lee, who was a colleague and close friend. That gave him an opportunity to become an authority on constitutional law.

By the time the Civil War began, Thomas was forty-five

General George H. Thomas, date unknown. This photograph was taken by Mathew Brady, one of the most important photographers of the Civil War period.

years old and affectionately known as Old Tom. A man of commanding presence, he was large and stout, about six feet tall, strong as an ox, with a serious face, kind eyes, and a winning smile. His beard was well trimmed and his face was weathered and bronzed from twenty years of service in the field. He had been promoted from lieutenant to captain to major to colonel and had vast experience and military expertise. His whole adult life had been spent in the army. No officer, in fact, was thought to know more about artillery and cavalry tactics, both of which he had taught at West Point. All of his hard-won experience and training made him a man of unusual value. When he chose to fight for the North, many were surprised, because he was Southern-born. Some members of President Lincoln's cabinet wondered if he could be trusted. Lincoln himself was doubtful. His old classmate William Tecumseh Sherman claimed he had to vouch for him, and told the following tale:

Mr. Lincoln, in the early part of the war, sent for me to come to Washington. While there he did me the honor to consult me regarding the names of those he intended to nominate to the Senate for brigadier generals. After hearing the proposed list I said to him, "Why don't you nominate old Thomas?" His reply was that Thomas was born in Virginia, and there were some doubts as to his loyalty. In my most earnest manner I protested indignantly against this most cruel accusation. I said: "Mr. President, Old Tom—as we always called him—is as loyal as I am, and as a soldier he is superior to all on your list." Mr. Lincoln said, "Will you be responsible for him?" and I unhesitating replied, "With the greatest pleasure." The President instantly sent his name among

General William Tecumseh Sherman, circa 1860s.

others to the Senate. In the afternoon of that day I went to the Senate Chamber to see my brother, John Sherman, of Ohio, and he told me of the names on the list of brigadier generals that had been sent to the Senate, and said they had all been confirmed, Thomas with the rest. I then began to recollect that I had not seen Thomas for twenty years, and I had become responsible for him. It was a hot day, and the thing so worried me that I went to the War Department and asked where Colonel Thomas, now brigadier general, was to be found. I was told, in Maryland, some eight or ten miles from the city. So I ordered a carriage and started at once, my anxiety to see him impelling me to urge the driver to make as rapid time as he could. When I arrived at the place I inquired where Colonel Thomas was; and the sergeant of the guard went with me to Thomas's tent, and found that he was in the saddle superintending some movement of the troops. Controlling my impatience, I waited in no easy frame of mind, that sultry day, for his return, and as there is an end to everything, Thomas came back at last and we greeted one another heartily. "Tom," said I, "you are a brigadier general." "I don't know of anyone that I would rather hear such news from than you," he replied. "But," I said, "Tom, there are some stories about your loyalty. How are you going?" "Billy," he replied, "I'm going South." "My God!" I exclaimed, "Tom, you have put me in an awful position; I have become responsible for your loyalty." "How so?" said he; so I related to him the conversation between President Lincoln and myself, when he leaned back, and remarked, "Give yourself no trouble, Billy; I am going South, but at the head of my men."

CHAPTER FIVE

THE WAR IN THE EAST
THE WAR IN THE WEST

The first major battle of the war had taken place in July 1861. A Union general by the name of Irvin McDowell had set out from Washington with 35,000 recruits to capture the important railroad junction of Manassas. He was opposed by an equal number of Southern troops under generals P. G. T. Beauregard and Joseph E. Johnston. On Sunday, July 21, the two armies met near a stream called Bull Run. Despite some Union blunders, the battle was fairly even, but then Confederate general Thomas J. Jackson stood like a stone wall and saved the day for the South. When the tide turned, Union forces panicked and ran. Many people had come down from Washington, D.C., with picnic baskets to watch the action. They perched themselves on hillsides at what they considered a safe distance and expected a quick Federal victory. Instead, they witnessed a mortifying, costly defeat. That had a sobering effect on the North.

Talk of a short war vanished. The three-month period of enlistment for which the first troops had volunteered was now over.

The new Federal army began to disappear. Congress authorized the calling up of half a million men for three years' volunteer service (as yet, there was no draft), and people settled down with grim determination to see the struggle through. McDowell was dismissed from his post as head of the army defending the capital and General George B. McClellan took command. No one was more qualified. He was only thirty-four, but his military career before the war had been brilliant. Now he took charge of all the Union armies, including the Army of the Potomac, which defended Washington, D.C.

As the volunteers began to stream in, McClellan drilled and trained them. The men learned how to carry, care for, and shoot their weapons; to wield the bayonet; to form into companies, battalions, and brigades; to pivot in and out of line in unison; and to execute field maneuvers as if under fire. By the spring of 1862, McClellan had created a splendid army of well over 100,000 men. The people of the North were eager to see this army used in a big, victorious campaign. But McClellan was determined not to do battle until he was sure he could win.

A depiction of the first great battle of the war, Bull Run, between the Federal army, commanded by Major General McDowell, and the Rebel army, under Generals Beauregard and Johnston, Sunday, July 21, 1861.

Some people saw McClellan as an American Napoleon — an all-conquering hero who would snuff out the rebellion and sweep its armies from the field. He saw himself that way, too, to some extent and did not always treat President Lincoln with proper respect. Lincoln overlooked his rudeness for the greater good. "I will hold McClellan's horse," he said, "if he will only bring us success."

Finally, Lincoln ordered McClellan to march on Richmond, the center of Southern resistance and the capital of the Confederate States. Instead of proceeding overland (a route fraught with danger), McClellan sensibly insisted on transporting his divided forces by water to Fort Monroe and to a point between the York and James rivers, in

General George B. McClellan, 1861.

Virginia. From there they marched westward up the peninsula toward Richmond.

General Joseph E. Johnston placed his smaller army of 60,000 in McClellan's path. As McClellan advanced, Johnston fell back slowly. Toward the end of May, near a place called Seven Pines, Johnston attacked. After a series of fierce battles, McClellan found himself outmaneuvered. He had come within sight of Richmond. But that was as far as he could go.

McClellan's campaign might have succeeded. But no sooner had he begun his march than the president's war council anxiously took 40,000 men from his army and arrayed them in defense of Washington, D.C. That made it impossible for McClellan to outflank the Rebel forces. He was bitterly disappointed. In anger, he telegraphed the secretary of war, Edwin M. Stanton: "I know that a few thousand more men would have changed this battle from

President Lincoln visits General McClellan at Antietam in September 1862.

a defeat to a victory. As it is, the government must not and cannot hold me responsible for the result. . . . If I save this army now, I tell you plainly that I owe no thanks to you or to any persons in Washington."

Stanton refused to accept that. Furious, he said, "If we gave McClellan a million men, he would sit down in the mud and yell for two."

On top of this defeat, Lincoln suffered a personal tragedy. During the first winter he was in the White House, his two little boys, Willie and Tad, one eleven years old and the other eight, fell ill. Tad recovered, but Willie's condition grew steadily worse. Lincoln spent all the time he could at the bedside of his child. But nothing could save him. When Willie died, Lincoln was overcome with grief and devoted himself all the more to his young son Tad. At the end of each day, Tad would come into his father's office, climb onto his lap, and tell him all he had been up to that day. Then he would fall asleep in his father's arms. The president would gently lay him down near his chair and go on with his work. When he had finished, he would gather Tad up, still sleeping, and carry him off to bed.

In the summer and fall of 1862, new battles were fought—the Second Battle of Bull Run, Antietam, and Fredericksburg. Neither side gained the upper hand. For every victory, there was also a defeat. One general after another was replaced. In contrast to this stalemate in the East, Union armies in the West gained ground. One objective there was to control the Tennessee and Cumberland rivers, which flowed south in somewhat parallel streams. Those rivers were crucial to transporting goods and weapons to the Western theater of the war for both sides. At a point where the rivers came by sweeping curves within a dozen miles of each other, the Confederates had built two strong

President Lincoln with his son Tad, circa 1865.

A fortified railroad bridge over the Cumberland River at Nashville, Tennessee, circa early 1860s.

forts, Fort Donelson on the Cumberland and Fort Henry on the Tennessee. Both were just south of the Kentucky line. Other Confederate forces were posted at Columbus, Mississippi, and Mill Springs, Kentucky.

Though Kentucky was a slave state, it had sided with the North—but not with a whole heart. A large portion of its population favored the South. So it was fertile ground for conflict. The Confederates hoped to take it, and both sides had troops within its borders. On January 19, 1862, General George H. Thomas defeated the Confederates at Mill Springs, gaining the first major Union victory in the

West. That breathed new life into the Union cause. Two weeks later, on February 6, General Ulysses S. Grant and a Union gunboat fleet under Admiral Andrew Foote took Fort Henry. The fight for Fort Donelson was harder, but it surrendered on February 15. Rebel strongholds on the upper Mississippi were also overrun, even as Union gunboats battered their way up from the mouth of the river to New Orleans. On March 7 and 8, a Rebel army that included 3,500 Indians was also beaten at Pea Ridge, Arkansas. As a result of all these gains, Missouri, northern Tennessee, and parts of Kentucky and Arkansas fell into Union hands.

After the fall of Fort Donelson, the Confederates pulled out of Nashville, Tennessee, which became a fortified supply

A lithograph of the Battle of Mill Springs, artist unknown.

General Ulysses S. Grant,
date unknown.

base for Union operations in the West. The evacuation of the city had been marked by scenes of panic, which the Rebel authorities helped create. An earthquake could not have shocked the city more. Women and children rushed madly through the streets screaming, "The Yankees are coming! The Yankees are coming!" Suitcases were thrown in haste from third-story windows and storehouses were looted by frantic mobs. One eyewitness reported seeing women and children slipping and sliding through the streets under loads of greasy pork they had stolen from a warehouse by the wharves. Departing Rebel troops also burned a beautiful suspension bridge that spanned the river by the town. By doing so, they hoped to prevent Union forces from mounting a pursuit.

The Confederates massed their troops at Corinth, Mississippi, just across the Tennessee line. Grant brought his troops up the Tennessee River to Pittsburg Landing, where he waited for another Union army under General Don Carlos Buell to join him. But before Buell got there, the Confederates attacked. Grant had failed to take any precautions—such as organizing his camp, entrenching his men in defensible positions, or posting a perimeter guard. He had even failed to heed clear warnings that the enemy was near. As a result, his army was almost destroyed. Soldiers were slaughtered while eating breakfast or were caught sleeping and stabbed to death in their beds. Thousands cowered in terror under bluffs by the river or fled into the woods. Only the arrival of Buell's army that evening prevented a complete disaster. The next day, the Federals pushed back and regained the ground they had lost. But their losses were severe. This was the famous Battle of Shiloh, named for the Shiloh Meeting House, a nearby Quaker church.

Grant was in disgrace. His poor generalship was a scandal, and many in the North wanted him dismissed. But Lincoln refused. He said, "I can't spare this man—he fights!"

Lincoln was a very great man and an excellent statesman. But as commander in chief, he made a number of mistakes. In the early days, he interfered too much with his field commanders, in that he second-guessed their better judgment, and failed to organize the

"The Yankees are coming! The Yankees are coming!"

nation for a long war. His ability to size up his generals correctly was also poor. When it came to picking the right ones, he was often at a loss. He admitted as much and once said that finding a good general was "like putting one's hand in a sack to get one eel from a dozen snakes." It is an awful irony of the war that he had so much concern for the welfare of the troops, yet sometimes gave a free hand to generals who were careless with their lives.

Sometimes he also gave too much weight to political considerations. This is one of the reasons both Ulysses S. Grant and William Tecumseh Sherman were able to advance as high as they did in the ranks of the army. In the whole course of the war, Sherman never won a battle, but his brother was a powerful senator from Ohio, and his father-in-law had been the nation's first secretary of the interior. Grant was from Lincoln's home state of Illinois and had a powerful advocate in Elihu Washburne, a congressman who had helped Lincoln get his party's presidential nomination. To be sure, Grant won some victories, however costly. He was also undoubtedly a feisty little man and full of "fight," as people said. But more was required of a first-rate general than that.

Yet in time a certain legend grew up around him and glamour clung to his name.

A painting of the Battle of Shiloh by Thure de Thulstrup, circa 1888.

There was little glamour in the common soldier's life. He carried his own haversack, blanket, rifle, ammunition, and canteen and lived on salt pork, pickled beef, hardtack, peas, and beans. The pickled beef (or "salt horse," as it was called) had to be soaked before eating; the salt pork was flabby and bland. The hardtack (large, thick crackers) was often infested with weevils and covered with mold. Pulverized peas sometimes served as a substitute for bread. Roots, leaves, buds, and even grass and weeds were simmered in a little water to serve as soup or broth. A soldier's stomach was rarely full. As one soldier put it, "We don't have more than half enough to eat."

It was the changing scenery—and often sheer excitement—of moving from place to place that gave army life its interest. It helped, too, that it brought together people from all walks of life. Some of the troops were farm boys, others street-smart urban kids. Some were well educated and knew the wider world; others came from homes so spare and rustic that they grew up using bits of stone for buttons and thorns for pins.

If their backgrounds were different, their hardships were the same. In camp, soldiers were done in by all sorts of diseases. In those days, even "children's diseases" like measles, mumps, and chicken pox could kill. Smallpox ate through the ranks. "There are new cases of smallpox

> "We don't have more than half enough to eat."

every day," one Union private wrote home to his mother. "As fast as one gets well another is taken. . . . I reckon," he added with grim humor, "there is as merry a set of fellows here as ever you saw, what there is left of us." Other diseases, like typhoid, dysentery, and pneumonia, were a death sentence from the start.

For the wounded, there was little the doctors could do. After any given battle,

Soldiers relax in front of their tent, 1861.

the moaning and sighing of the wounded and dying was so heartrending as to cause any man to oppose war. Limbs and body parts of all kinds were strewn about, and in places the dead were stacked like cordwood in the yards. Some lay with their tongues swelled out of their mouths, others with their hands stuck out as if surprised, with an expression of amazement on their faces.

When the wounded were brought in, doctors and surgeons got to work cutting and carving like butchers. "It is redicklous how bad they is taken care of," complained one

A hospital carriage picks up the wounded on the battlefield, circa early 1860s.

soldier. Another, speaking of a dying friend, said, "I don't believe he could have suffered any more if he had been burnt up." In fact, doctors often made things worse. They had no idea yet of common hygiene, didn't wash their hands, and went from one patient to another with fingers soaked in pus. In those days, they thought the appearance of pus in a wound was a positive sign.

"One good cook is worth ten doctors," it was said.

"One good cook is worth ten doctors."

The new weaponry of the war—especially more accurate, high-powered rifles, with bullets that spread on contact, shattering cartilage and bone—made almost any wound deadly. In that sense, the rifle was an entirely new technological development, fundamentally different from the old-fashioned muskets used during (and since) the Revolutionary War. Sometimes raw troops were also sent into combat before they had even been trained. Heartbreak abounded. Here is a letter one Illinois farm boy wrote home from Perryville, Kentucky, after he had buried his teenage brother on the field:

This is the soldier who wrote the Perryville Battle Ground letter. His name was Benjamin Webb Baker and he is the great-grandfather of the author of this book.

Perryville Battle Ground,
Oct. 11, 1862.

Oh Mother; How can I say it! But I must!! John is dead!!! He was killed on the battlefield on the 8th in one of the hottest engagements of the war—he was shot in two places. The balls must have struck him at the same instant—one entered his left side at the waistband & passing through his heart came out under his right arm. The other struck him in the neck under the jaw & near the jugular vein & passed up into his brain. Either of the balls would have killed him instantly. He evidently never moved after he fell, nor at all only to fall for his arms were as if he had been holding his gun to shoot. I suppose he was at the time the balls struck him. I was on the right of the battle field and he on the left. I did not know that he was on the field at all till the next day. There was only a skirmish on the right—but on the left it was very hot. Crocket Neal [a friend from home] was killed

half a mile from the line of battle in the retreat. I suppose a stray ball must have struck him. It went into the back of his head & did not pass through. He fell on his face & apparently never moved. Anthony Cox [another friend] was killed. Anthony was shot through both legs just above the knees. The legs were both broken. He was not killed instantly, but doubtless soon bled to death. He must have suffered. He attempted to crawl off the field — he got back about 8 or 10 feet from where he fell. There was an agony look on his face. . . . I send you a lock of John's hair. Everything was taken from his pockets but his Testament. John died like a man & a soldier at his post & in the front rank. Would I had died in his stead — my only, my true & noble hearted brother. What a great vicarious sacrifice our homes & country are costing. How many noble hearted brothers. I can't write more. God bless & sustain you in this great bereavement. . . . Truly your son.

No one can read a letter like this without tasting the bitterness of war.

For the most part, the best a soldier could hope for was to keep busy — reading when he could (if he could — a large number of soldiers were illiterate), mending his clothes, or playing games like checkers or cards. Still better was a good march. As one soldier put it when he went into camp for a time in Mississippi: "I would rather go [march] every day even if we only went 10 miles & back, so they would make us believe we were going some place. I get so lazy laying in camp — I am sure to get the blues." Boredom increased as the temperature rose. The days seemed to pass by in a haze. "The boys are in their tents or shelters from the scorching rays of the sun," he told his mother, "for I tell you it does scorch down here. . . . We get up at 3 a.m., get breakfast & scrape & clean our tents and yards & ground & then drill an hour & a half—that brings us to 6 a.m. By that time it is so hot that we hunt the shade till evening when we have supper, drill and dress parade. This is all we do. . . . We count it a killing job."

Not surprisingly, many deserted from both sides. Deserters turned up everywhere, in towns and cities, in the woods and on lonely roads. It was often impossible to tell which side they had fought for, or deserted from. One day, after a battle, a Confederate general and his staff encountered a hobo on a mule. The man was barefoot and unkempt, with an unwashed face and a tangled beard. As the general rode up, the hobo took out a corncob pipe and calmly began to smoke.

"This is all we do. . . . We count it a killing job."

"Who are you?" asked the general.

"Nobody," said the man.

"Where did you come from?"

"Nowhere."

"Where are you going?"

"I don't know."

"Aren't you a Confederate soldier?"

"What might that be?"

In exasperation, the general turned and galloped away.

For a wanderer to behave like that toward a general was risky, for he might have been shot or hanged on the spot. It was safer for most deserters (at least from the South) to surrender to the other side. One day five Confederate deserters encountered a Union private bathing in a river. They ordered him out at gunpoint, and the private thought he was done for. After he had put his clothes on, one of the Confederates said: "You're a Yankee, right?"

"Yes."

"Do you surrender?"

"Of course I do."

"Great! Now, we'll surrender to you!" And the five stacked their arms and demanded the Union private "surround them" and take them to his camp.

Yet to be a prisoner of war could be a dreadful thing. There were some terrible prisons in the North. But the worst were in the South. And the most terrible of all was a place called Andersonville. Andersonville was a prison camp in Georgia run by a sadist by the name of Captain Wirz. The camp was situated in a huge field of about twenty acres and was enclosed by a stockade. In the middle of the field was a swamp, where more than 30,000 prisoners were confined.

Andersonville prison, 1864.

There was no shelter from sun, wind, or rain, and prisoners were compelled to burrow like wild animals in the earth. The conditions were unspeakable, without sanitation of any kind, and the men died of starvation and disease. Some were literally eaten up by maggots. Others were tortured or shot without excuse. Quite a few went mad. It was not uncommon for a prisoner to make a break for it in order to be shot—just so his misery would end. No one knows how many prisoners died in Southern camps, but over 10,000 died in Andersonville alone.

On the whole, the better any given army was run, the less likely its men were to be killed or captured, or to desert. The Union and Confederate armies consisted of many armies, in fact, with names drawn from the area or landscape where they were deployed. Most Union armies were named after streams or rivers—the Army of the Potomac, for example, or the Army of the Cumberland (named for the Cumberland River). Most Confederate armies were named after regions or states—the Army of Northern Virginia, for example, or the Army of Tennessee. Each army had its own character or style. No army was better managed than the Army of the Cumberland, which General George H. Thomas led. One fellow officer recalled: "Next to the Army of the Potomac, the Army of the Cumberland was the largest Union Army in the field. It was also the most compact, the most complete in all its departments, the most thoroughly disciplined and organized. Its esprit de corps was equaled by none. It worked like a machine, it lived like a family, it had the soul of honor. From head to foot there were neither malice, jealousies, plottings and intrigues." In short, it reflected (as most armies do) the character of the man at its helm.

Thomas saw to it that the food the men ate was often fresh and introduced such items as canned tomatoes into

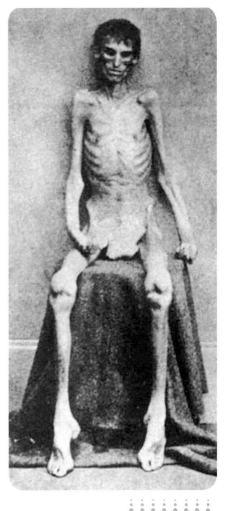

A survivor of the cruel conditions at Andersonville prison.

A soldier's drawing of troops sharing rations, date unknown.

their diet. Good portable baking ovens were in every camp, and the entire army, which numbered on average about 65,000, was supplied with fresh bread four days a week. Sauerkraut and pickles were stored in enormous barrels and helped prevent scurvy, a vitamin-deficiency disease. (Scurvy was awful, causing joint pains, swollen gums, and the teeth to fall out.)

The amount of food consumed by the army was immense. When it was stationed in middle Tennessee, for example, 300 tons of provisions of all kinds came in by freight train every day. To keep the army warm for just one winter, whole forests were cut down and 18,000 cords of wood were burned.

The medical care in Thomas's army was as good as one could get. His field hospitals were towns unto themselves. The one at Murfreesboro, Tennessee, was almost a city of tents, with broad streets and alleyways with gutters on each side. Above the gutters were sidewalks made of planks. In the town itself, Thomas chose the largest and best-ventilated buildings for care of the sick. The walls were whitened, the floors thoroughly scoured, and neat cot bedsteads ranged in exact lines through the long rooms. The mattresses were all filled with fresh straw and topped with crisp white sheets, clean new blankets, and a soft pillow. Altogether in his Medical Department, Thomas had 35 general hospitals staffed by 400 surgeons and 3,000 nurses and attendants. After a battle, there were 600 ambulances (in those days, horse-driven covered wagons) ready to pick up the wounded on the field.

"Its [Army of the Cumberland] esprit de corps was equaled by none. It worked like a machine, it lived like a family, it had the soul of honor. From head to foot there were neither malice, jealousies, plottings and intrigues."

One of the "tent cities" of the Army of the Potomac, Virginia, May 1862.

A soldier's world was hard. So it is not surprising that Thomas was idolized by his men not only for his great generalship but for his humane attention to their needs. Indeed, it was admitted (even by those jealous of Thomas) that his men regarded him with something like love.

CHAPTER SEVEN

CARNAGE

The war effort faltered. In the East, George B. McClellan was replaced as head of the Army of the Potomac by General John Pope, then Pope was replaced by Ambrose Burnside, then Burnside by "Fighting Joe" Hooker in January 1863. Hooker restored morale and brought Union strength back up to 134,000 men. On April 4, Lincoln visited Hooker's headquarters. One of the soldiers who saw Lincoln that afternoon wrote: "None of us to our dying day can forget that countenance! Concentrated in that one great, strong, yet tender face, the agony of the life-or-death struggle was revealed as we had never seen it before. With new understanding we knew why we were soldiers."

Yet even under great strain, Lincoln was never at a loss for a humorous remark. One day, in a crowded hospital, it was whispered from cot to cot that Lincoln was in the building and would soon pass by. All who could do so stood up, ready to salute.

> "None of us to our dying day can forget that countenance! Concentrated in that one great, strong, yet tender face, the agony of the life-or-death struggle was revealed as we had never seen it before. With new understanding we knew why we were soldiers."

Among them was a soldier from Pennsylvania who was six feet, seven inches tall. That made him three inches taller than Lincoln himself. When Lincoln approached him, he

63

Confederate dead behind the stone wall of Marye's Heights, Fredericksburg, Virginia, circa early 1860s.

stopped and looked the soldier up and down in amazement. Then he grasped his hand and said, "Hello, comrade. How do you know when your feet get cold?"

A month later, Hooker crossed the Rappahannock River and advanced against Robert E. Lee, the seemingly invincible head of the Army of Northern Virginia. As Hooker passed through an area known as the Wilderness, made up of thick woods and dense undergrowth, Lee outflanked him and beat him badly at a place called Chancellorsville. The fighting lasted for three days and extended over an area of ten miles. The carnage was awful, and Lincoln near despair. "My God! My God!" he cried. "What will the country say!"

It was one of the darkest periods of the war. The North was dismayed. The war had cost tens of thousands of lives, and it was costing the country a fortune in money each day. Yet there was almost nothing to show for it in the way of success. Even in the West, the contest for Kentucky and Tennessee had been renewed. Major battles were fought at Perryville and Stones River, but defeated Rebel armies escaped to fight another day.

When the war had begun, volunteers had come forward in large numbers. So many had volunteered, in fact, that thousands were turned away. But before the end of the second year, the war had grown so unpopular and its eventual outcome so doubtful that volunteering had almost ceased. Men lost heart. In March 1863, Congress authorized a draft, which affected all able-bodied male citizens between the ages of twenty and forty-five. Riots broke out in opposition to it. But the draft was enforced.

In the East, Robert E. Lee now boldly advanced through Maryland into Pennsylvania to threaten Northern supply lines, gather provisions, and strengthen Confederate morale by going on offense. Hooker almost at once was replaced by General George Gordon Meade, and his army met Lee's at the little Pennsylvania town of Gettysburg. It was an epic fight. The climax of the battle came on the afternoon of

A drawing of the draft lottery in New York City.

Draft riots in New York City, 1863.

An 1863 wood engraving by Theodore R. Davis showing the surrender at Vicksburg.

July 3, when Confederate general George E. Pickett led a fruitless charge against the center of the Union line. By the time the battle ended, 51,000 men had fallen on both sides and the fields were soaked in blood.

Lee had risked too much. But Meade failed to catch Lee's army as it withdrew. On the same day, July 4, 1863, there

was an important development in the West, when Vicksburg, on the Mississippi, finally surrendered to Grant after a long siege. The whole of the Mississippi River was now in Union hands. Lincoln exclaimed: "The Father of Waters now rolls unvexed to the sea."

But the victory came at great cost. It had involved the

unnecessary deaths of thousands, many of whom perished of disease in the swamps. Others, wounded, were left to bake to death in the sun because Grant was too stubborn to ask for a truce. In the end, he won simply because his army was larger and because the starving defenders were reduced to eating bugs and rats.

On the battlefield of Gettysburg, the fallen soldiers of both sides were buried on Cemetery Ridge. This spot, made sacred by the sacrifice of so many lives, was set apart as a national cemetery. On the day appointed for its consecration, a vast company assembled to honor the occasion. Lincoln was there, and said a few words. He stood for a moment and gazed out at the audience in silence. Then, in his high treble voice, he delivered one of the greatest speeches of all time:

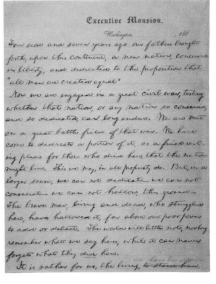

Lincoln's first draft of the Gettysburg Address.

Four score and seven years ago our fathers brought forth, upon this continent, a new nation, conceived in liberty, and dedicated to the proposition that all men are created equal. Now we are engaged in a great civil war, testing whether that nation, or any nation so conceived and so dedicated, can long endure. We are met on a great battlefield of that war. We have come to dedicate a portion of that field, as a final resting place for those who here gave their lives that that nation might live. It is altogether fitting and proper that we should do this. But, in a larger sense, we cannot dedicate—we cannot consecrate—we cannot hallow—this ground. The brave men, living and dead, who struggled here, have consecrated it, far above our poor power to add or detract. The world will little note, nor long remember what we say here, but it can never forget what they did here. It is for us, the living, rather to be dedicated here to the unfinished work which they who fought here have thus far so nobly advanced. It is rather for us to be here dedicated to the great task remaining before us, that from these honored dead we take increased devotion to that cause for which they gave the last full measure of devotion; that we here highly resolve that these dead shall not have died in vain; that this nation, under God, shall have a new birth of freedom, and that this government of the people, by the people, and for the people shall not perish from this earth.

While Grant was accepting the surrender of Vicksburg, Federal armies were pushing forward in middle Tennessee. They evicted the Confederates from Tullahoma, crossed the Tennessee River, and closed in on the key city of Chattanooga, the gateway to the South. When the Confederates withdrew into Georgia, the Federals followed in a chase. In doing so, they fell into a trap. The Confederates had pretended to retreat but instead took up a position just over the Georgia line by a creek known as Chickamauga, which in the language of the Cherokee Indians means "River of Death." This brought about a desperate battle (September 19–20, 1863) in which the Federal army came within a hairsbreadth of defeat. When the Rebels broke through a gap in the Federal line, most of the Federal army fled in panic back to Chattanooga. Only General George H. Thomas and his troops remained on the field to make a stand. In what Lincoln himself called the greatest instance of courage "in the history of the world," Thomas and his remaining men repelled one onslaught after another of the entire Confederate army. Eventually, at nightfall, Thomas withdrew to Chattanooga. That led to the more elaborate Battle of Chattanooga in November, which the Federals won.

The Union victory at Chattanooga opened the way for an invasion of the South. But the South still had two large, strong armies in the field. These were General Robert E. Lee's Army of Northern Virginia and a combined force under General Joseph E. Johnston at Dalton, Georgia. The great strategic front that Jefferson Davis, the Confederate president, had once drawn from Mississippi to Virginia had been broken in a number of places. But it was not beyond repair.

At this juncture, the armies of the North were joined together in a coordinated plan. In the past, they had often moved out of step with one another, "like a team of balky horses," as General Ulysses S. Grant put it. Now they were to work together as one. On March 3, 1864, Grant was summoned by telegraph to the War Office in Washington, and there, on March 9, President Abraham Lincoln, in the presence of his cabinet, made him general in chief. In a brief statement, Lincoln commended Grant for what he had done—or was believed to have done, at the battles at Fort Henry and Fort Donelson, Vicksburg, and Chattanooga—and for what he expected him to do. In reply, Grant promised, with the help of Providence, not to disappoint Lincoln's expectations.

Soon after that, Grant came up with a new strategy to win the war. Grant himself was to advance against Lee and destroy him, taking the Confederate capital of Richmond, Virginia, if he could. At the same time, his close friend and fellow general William Tecumseh Sherman would advance against Johnston's army, arrayed in defense of Atlanta, Georgia, and bring it to bay. Both Grant and Sherman hoped to cut their opponents' supply lines and force them to fight the Union army face to face. Grant intended to do this by a hammering force; Sherman, by a wide wheeling movement through the South that took advantage of all the Union army's Western gains. In a letter to Sherman on April 4, Grant told him not only to "break up" Johnston's army but to inflict what damage he could on his resources—in short, to destroy his capacity to make war.

But all this failed to work out as planned.

An 1888 painting of the Battle of Chattanooga, artist unknown. This great battle, ultimately won by General George H. Thomas, was viewed by many (including Jefferson Davis) as a turning point of the war.

It was this series of events that had brought Lincoln to Grant's headquarters at City Point, Virginia, in the summer of 1864 to talk about the war.

Grant's strategy had ultimately brought his own huge army, after many battles often marked by useless slaughter, to a stalemate with Lee's army before Petersburg, Virginia. By the end of the summer, he had lost 60,000 men.

Behind closed doors in the White House, even Lincoln's wife called Grant a butcher.

The outlook was bleak.

Meanwhile, Sherman was marching to Atlanta but, in a bungled campaign, would fail to destroy his opponent. Opposed to Sherman was General Joseph Johnston and his tough, veteran Army of Tennessee. Johnston's army, encamped at Dalton, Georgia, astride the Atlanta-Chattanooga Railroad, was 53,000 strong—about half as large as Sher-

A Harper's Weekly *illustration (June 4, 1864) of the engagement at Snake Creek Gap, Georgia.*

man's but able to retreat from one fortified line to another as Sherman advanced. That advance proved costly and was drawn out for several months. It turned into "one big Indian fight," as Sherman complained. It could have been won at the outset if Sherman had adopted a plan put forward by Thomas to move a large force through a place called Snake Creek Gap. That would have enabled Sherman to outflank (that is, get around) the Confederates and get a part of his army behind the Confederate line. Instead, Sherman engaged in a series of head-on assaults on the strong Confederate position, which included a range of steep, rocky cliffs. Finally, Sherman realized that what he was doing was tantamount to suicide for his army and sent troops through Snake Creek Gap—as Thomas had urged at the start. But Sherman was too late. He also used a force too small for the task. The Confederate army escaped.

As the North lost more and more men, more drafts were levied to meet the army's manpower needs. By late 1864, the shocking losses on the battlefield, especially by Grant's army in Virginia, had drastically depleted Union ranks. Finally, on September 2, Sherman's army captured Atlanta. That was just in time to ease the gloom in the North enough to get Lincoln reelected to a second term as president.

n August 1864, the Confederate command in the West had been transferred to John Bell Hood. A big man with a long, sad face and languid, drooping eyes, Hood was a stand-up fighter and always ready for a brawl. He was something of a hothead, but relentless. That was both his weakness and his strength. He was fearless—therefore, to be feared. He had lost the use of an arm at the Battle of Gettysburg and had lost a leg at Chickamauga. When he rode into battle, he had to be strapped to the saddle of his horse. Some wondered if his mind was right, or if it had been impaired by all the drugs he took for his pain. But he was a gallant soldier. No one doubted that. And his veteran army was incredibly tough.

Serving as his cavalry commander was Nathan Bedford Forrest, the best in the Confederate army. Forrest was not only wily, but ruthless. He had slaughtered a garrison of black soldiers who tried to surrender in one of the worst atrocities of the war. After the war, he would become the first Grand Wizard of the Ku Klux Klan.

While Sherman was resting his army in occupied Atlanta, Hood evaded capture and moved northwestward into Alabama and Tennessee. Instead of trying to catch him, Sherman embarked on his famous March to the Sea. This was a campaign of wanton devastation to the Atlantic seacoast in which towns and crops were burned. It was aimed not at destroying an army—Sherman had failed to do that—but at destroying the enemy's will. Sherman had little reason to expect any real resistance. After

General John Bell Hood, date unknown.

all, each day's march would carry him further away from Hood. Yet he took with him over 60,000 men, the cream of the great army that General George H. Thomas (Sherman's co-commander) had built up in the West. He could do that because Grant had placed Sherman in overall command in that theater of the war. That left Thomas with just 25,000 men to deal with Hood. Thomas decided to make Nashville the center of his new defense line. Hood collected more men and supplies and hoped to take Nashville before Thomas could make it strong.

If Hood prevailed against Thomas or got past him, there was nothing to stop him from marching on to the Ohio River, then down into Virginia, to help Lee beat Grant.

Suddenly the whole outcome of the war seemed at stake.

Starting from Chattanooga, Thomas made his way to Nashville, with Hood not far behind. At Nashville, Thomas assembled another 35,000 men, largely drawn from other commands. Some of these newfound troops were also Sherman's "rejects," including convalescents and malingerers, as well as raw recruits and untried companies of blacks. As he put his patchwork army together—and prepared to battle an army Sherman himself had said couldn't be destroyed— the authorities in Washington (Grant included) grew impatient and threatened to strip him of command. They wanted Thomas to grapple with Hood before he was ready—even before some of his troops had arrived. But Thomas would not be rushed.

One of Grant's military maxims was that there comes a point in every great battle where both sides are exhausted to the point of defeat. Whoever strikes first then wins. This was a very crude idea of military tactics. It ignored the time-honored

General Nathan Bedford Forrest, date unknown.

virtues of outsmarting an opponent by fighting battles in a shrewd, clever, or scientific way. But it conformed to Grant's idea of a battle as a slugfest, which is how his battles were often fought. Nor did Grant believe much in strategy. "The art of war is simple enough," Grant once said. "Find out where your enemy is. Get at him as soon as you can. Strike at him hard as you can, and keep moving on."

"The art of war is simple enough," Grant once said. "Find out where your enemy is. Get at him as soon as you can. Strike at him hard as you can, and keep moving on."

It has been claimed that Grant had drive. But any general with a surplus of men can keep going. It was not Grant's own determination or will that gave him strength. It was what he could afford. He had the manpower to spend and he would spend it. Unlike Lee, he knew he could replenish what he lost. The North had a huge manpower advantage. So Grant was ready, willing, and able to spend two men for every one Lee lost. Why did Lincoln go along with this? He didn't, exactly. But he had promised Grant a free hand. He told him to develop his plans, but he also told him he didn't need to know what they were. Early in the war, Lincoln had sometimes erred by trying to micromanage his commanders. Now, to a large extent, he surrendered civilian oversight of the war.

That proved to be deeply unwise.

Thomas was a different kind of general. He knew what it cost to make a soldier and what that soldier was worth after he was made. He therefore insisted on some positive advantage for every drop of blood shed. He poured his men into battle only when it counted; and when it counted, he prevailed. He had given the Union its first major victory in the West at Mill Springs, Kentucky, which helped open the way to Tennessee. He had held the center at Stones River, where, on a wooded knoll known afterward as Hell's Half Acre, he snatched victory from defeat. He had saved the day at Chickamauga (the most ferocious battle of the war), where on the crest of Horseshoe Ridge he withstood the repeated assaults of the whole Rebel army. Thereafter, Thomas was known as the Rock of Chickamauga—against which the wild waves of battle dashed in vain. Thomas and his army had also done the bulk of the hard fighting during Sherman's Atlanta campaign. In the end, it could be said of him, and him alone, that he never lost a battle. In the course of the war, he also destroyed two Confederate armies and saved two Union armies from destruction by his own personal valor and skill.

In his military planning, Thomas was always thorough. In that way, he was conventional in the best sense. But in other ways, his thinking was advanced. For example, he helped introduce the use of map coordinates into battle planning, developed the portable pontoon bridge (a flotation device that allowed troops to march across rivers), improvised a mobile field hospital system, and created the first mobile command post.

All this helped to make the art of war a more technologically up-to-date enterprise.

Some of the most memorable words of the war were Thomas's, too. After the first day's battle at Stones River, in Tennessee, when it looked as if the Union army might be beaten, the commanding general, William S. Rosecrans, called a midnight council of war. He met with his other generals in a cabin in the woods. Their staff officers also crowded in. Rosecrans was seated on a stool, drying his clothes, which were still splattered with the blood and brains of his chief of staff, who had been beheaded by a cannonball. The officers were dirty, powder-stained, weary, and depressed. One officer recalled, "If there was a cheerful face present I did not see it." But turning to Thomas, he saw him "as always, calm, stern, determined, silent, and perfectly self-possessed, his hat set squarely on his head. It was inspiring to look at the man."

A grim half hour of silence passed as raindrops pelted the clapboard roof.

Finally, Rosecrans asked each of his generals in turn, "Should we attack tomorrow or retreat?" He went around the room. One by one, they said, "Retreat." Then he came to Thomas. Thomas frowned and rose slowly to his feet. He buttoned his greatcoat from bottom to top, faced his fellow officers, and said, "Gentlemen, this army can't retreat! I know of no better place to die than right here," and walked out of the room into the night.

Over the course of the next few days, the army made its stand and won.

When Thomas was at Chattanooga and his army under siege, Grant sent a message to him that read: "Hold Chattanooga at all hazards," meaning, at all costs. Thomas replied promptly: "We will hold Chattanooga till we starve." In the

> But turning to Thomas, he saw him "as always, calm, stern, determined, silent, and perfectly self-possessed, his hat set squarely on his head. It was inspiring to look at the man."

series of battles that followed, Thomas and his army did the major part. He approved one force going up Lookout Mountain to win the famous Battle Above the Clouds and another up Missionary Ridge. That remarkable charge—straight uphill against entrenched Confederate positions—succeeded against all odds and won the day. The assistant secretary of war Charles A. Dana, who witnessed the charge, called it "a miracle of God."

A soldier's drawing of Missionary Ridge before the battle.

It was the second time in the war that Thomas had shattered a Rebel army in the field.

Grant was not happy about that, though as the general in charge he got credit for the triumph. But he resented Thomas and viewed him as a rival. He had done so ever since his own disgrace at Shiloh, when he had failed to guard against the Rebel attack. As a result of that battle, he had been removed from the command of his own army and Thomas was put in his place. That arrangement lasted for only a short time, and Thomas had nothing to do with it. But Grant never forgot it. He had a "jealous" nature, as Navy Secretary Gideon Welles put it, and proved hostile toward anyone who was not his acolyte. Since then, with the connivance of Sherman, who proved a false friend, he had disparaged Thomas behind his back. He had also lobbied against Thomas's promotions and done everything he could to limit his reputation and rank.

Thomas, by contrast, was a man of honor through and through. He was a soldier's soldier and in every way manly, yet also noble, gracious, and refined. His men revered him and yearned for his approval and respect. That is one reason they fought so well under his eye. Like Lincoln, he also had a wise and gentle heart. By nature, he took the part of the helpless and could not bear the sight of unnecessary suffering in man or beast. He was kind to animals, and around his tent could always be found stray dogs and cats he had picked up. One day in camp, some officers captured a goose at a nearby farm and were preparing to kill it. The goose escaped and they chased it all about in a shower of feathers. Finally, Thomas came roaring out of his tent. Honking softly, the goose circled once more in the air, landed, and waddled over to where Thomas stood. There it settled at his feet. The goose looked up, Thomas looked down, and the goose became a mascot of the camp.

At his headquarters at Nashville, one pet or another could always be found trailing behind him as he went about his tasks.

CHAPTER NINE

THE BATTLE OF NASHVILLE

After Sherman left Atlanta in flames and began marching through Georgia—in a slash-and-burn campaign largely waged against the civilian population—Hood's army, in Tennessee, waited for supplies and reinforcements to come up from Mississippi and Alabama by train. At Nashville, Thomas did all he could to prepare for the onslaught he knew was coming. Most of the troops he had were then posted at Pulaski, Tennessee, under General John Schofield, his second in command.

Hood's army was energized. Hood himself had put the disappointments of the Atlanta campaign behind him and, despite a body crippled by wounds, dashed about in the saddle like a man possessed. As a general, he was "ready to risk all on the casting of a die."

His army was strong and was arranged in three corps, commanded by generals S. D. Lee, Benjamin Cheatham, and Alexander Stewart—all tried and true. Each corps contained three divisions. With a cavalry force of 10,000 to 15,000, Hood had a tightly knit veteran army of 55,000 men.

Meanwhile, Grant's military machine, including the Grand Army of the Potomac, as it was called, lay immobilized before Petersburg, Virginia, as Sherman's vast legions disappeared from view. Lincoln didn't even know where Sherman's troops were. He said to his secretary of war, "I know what hole he went in at, but I can't tell what hole he will come out of." Too late, Grant and Sherman realized that their own wild strategy of ignoring Hood's army might prove a huge mistake.

In the Civil War, the chief strategic objectives—aside from capturing the enemy's capital—were to defeat or destroy the opposing army or force it to retreat; to seize strategic sites (supply lines, depots, arsenals, communications centers, and industries) important to the war effort; to damage the enemy's economy; and to exhaust his will to fight. In the Western theater of the war, all these objectives were suddenly within Hood's reach.

The nation waited in suspense.

As Hood began building bridges for his offensive, Thomas told Schofield to fall back toward Nashville so as not to be trapped by flanking movements as Hood advanced. Schofield, however (who was not much of a general), was almost surrounded at Pulaski

THE BATTLE OF NASHVILLE

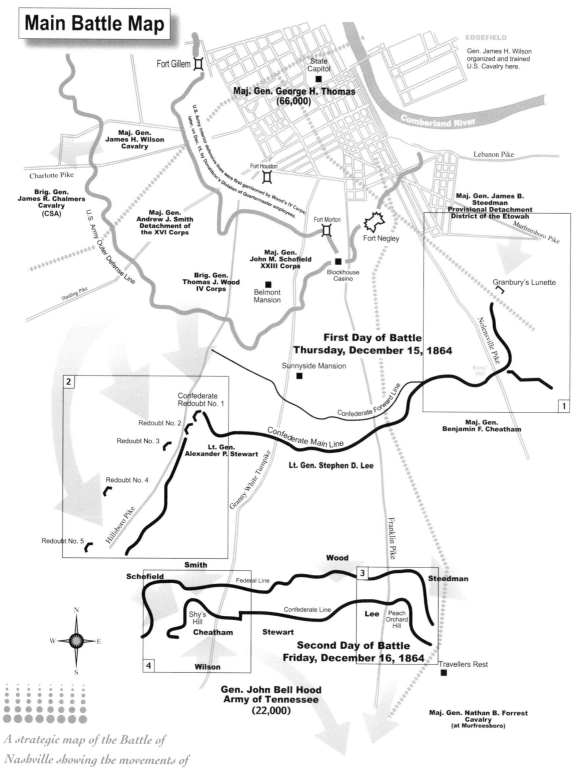

Main Battle Map

Fort Gillem

EDGEFIELD

Gen. James H. Wilson organized and trained U.S. Cavalry here.

State Capitol

Maj. Gen. George H. Thomas (66,000)

Cumberland River

Lebanon Pike

Maj. Gen. James H. Wilson Cavalry

U.S. Army interior defense lines were first garrisoned by Wood's IV Corps; later, on Dec. 15, by Donaldson's Division of Quartermaster employees.

Charlotte Pike

Fort Houston

Maj. Gen. James B. Steedman Provisional Detachment District of the Etowah

Brig. Gen. James R. Chalmers Cavalry (CSA)

Maj. Gen. Andrew J. Smith Detachment of the XVI Corps

Fort Morton

Fort Negley

Murfreesboro Pike

U.S. Army Outer Defense Line

Maj. Gen. John M. Schofield XXIII Corps

Blockhouse Casino

Granbury's Lunette

Brig. Gen. Thomas J. Wood IV Corps

Belmont Mansion

Harding Pike

Nolensville Pike

Sunnyside Mansion

First Day of Battle Thursday, December 15, 1864

Rams' Hill

Confederate Forward Line

2

Confederate Redoubt No. 1

Redoubt No. 2

Redoubt No. 3

Confederate Main Line

1

Lt. Gen. Alexander P. Stewart

Maj. Gen. Benjamin F. Cheatham

Redoubt No. 4

Lt. Gen. Stephen D. Lee

Granny White Turnpike

Redoubt No. 5

Franklin Pike

Hillsboro Pike

Smith

Wood

Schofield

Federal Line

3

Steedman

Shy's Hill

Confederate Line

Lee

Peach Orchard Hill

N
W E
S

Cheatham

Stewart

4

Wilson

Second Day of Battle Friday, December 16, 1864

Travellers Rest

Gen. John Bell Hood Army of Tennessee (22,000)

Maj. Gen. Nathan B. Forrest Cavalry (at Murfreesboro)

A strategic map of the Battle of Nashville showing the movements of both the Union and Confederate troops.

and nearly captured at Spring Hill. That brought him to Franklin.

Thomas did all he could to buy time. Promised troops had yet to arrive. Reinforcements—a corps of troops under A. J. Smith—were on their way from Missouri. Many of those at Nashville were still not up to speed. As Thomas worked furiously to fortify the outskirts of the city, Hood hoped to overtake Schofield on a bend of the Harpeth River, just eighteen miles away, and destroy him before he could cross. Expecting Hood's attack at any time, Schofield repaired a bridge, took refuge himself on the far side of the river, and arranged his troops in a wedge. He had barely done so when Hood arrived. It would prove a bloody day. On November 30, Hood hurled part of his army across mile-wide open fields without artillery support against Schofield's defenses. Hood took some heavy losses, but forced Schofield to retreat. The area where the fiercest fighting took place looked like "a slaughter pen."

Schofield had escaped destruction by the skin of his teeth. Back at Nashville, Thomas knew how much danger Schofield was in. All that day, he had been "reticent and gloomy," with his military hat pulled down low over his grave gray eyes. But after Schofield's corps survived, "his hat lifted, his broad brow cleared, and his strong and massive face began to shine."

Schofield arrived in Nashville on the night of December 1 with Hood on his heels. By then, Thomas had established two fortified defense lines, one behind the other, enveloping the city along the Cumberland River from bank to bank. Studding these lines were earthen redoubts (or small forts), which he labored without rest to connect and make strong. Three large forts anchored the city's defense works—the largest being Fort Negley on St. Cloud Hill. It had two

A southwest view of Fort Negley. The first shots of the battle were fired from here.

massive, bombproof bastions and eleven heavy guns, including a cannon known as a Parrott rifle that could hurl a twenty-nine-pound shell more than two miles.

Meanwhile, the troops Thomas had been waiting for at last came in, including the troops from Missouri by steamboat and black regiments from Chattanooga that rumbled in on the rails. When A. J. Smith, a big bear of a man like Thomas, came striding in, Thomas was so glad to see him he literally took him in his arms and embraced him. At one o'clock that morning, with his fellow generals looking on, Thomas explained, with maps spread out on the floor, the upcoming battle he had planned.

In just a few weeks, Thomas had made an army. Some of the troops were raw. Others, like those belonging to Smith, were hardened veterans of many a fight. One officer encountered a group of Smith's men camped out along the river and asked them who they were. "We're A. J. Smith's guerrillas," one man replied. "We've been to Vicksburg, Red River, Missouri, and about everywhere else . . . and now we're going to Hell."

At Nashville, Thomas had made the most of what he had. As he arrayed his troops on the heights about the city, he placed an improvised division, including regiments of blacks on the left, cavalry on the right, and the rest in between. Schofield's corps was held in reserve to be used where needed as the battle played out. The interior (or second) line of Nashville's defense was manned largely by armed civilian employees. Union gunboats patrolled the Cumberland River above and below the city to prevent the Rebels from getting across.

In putting black soldiers on the front lines around Nashville, Thomas was doing something daring for the time. At the beginning of the war, blacks had not been allowed to serve in the Union ranks. Many Northern troops were still too prejudiced to accept it. And Lincoln, after all, had not gone to war to abolish slavery but to keep the Union intact. Three slave states, in fact—Maryland, Delaware, and Ken-

Black Union soldiers, 1865. General George H. Thomas was the only Union general to give black troops an important role in a major battle of the war.

tucky—had remained in the Union, and a fourth, Missouri, had been kept in by force. Lincoln had hoped these states would voluntarily free their slaves. But in his public policy toward emancipation (the idea that all slaves should be freed), Lincoln had remained cautious, for he was afraid to antagonize those who had volunteered to fight only for the principle of majority rule. But the longer the war dragged on, the more emancipation made political and military sense.

For one thing, the sentiment in Europe against slavery was very strong, and Lincoln wanted the people of Europe on his side. That would make it less likely that any European power would intervene on the Confederacy's behalf. At the same time, emancipation would enlarge the Union army. The Confederates were using slaves to do all kinds of work—digging ditches, repairing railroad tracks, and so on—to help their forces. If these slaves could be freed by Union troops, the workforce of the South would be reduced and ex-slaves who wished to could fight for the North.

Of course, throughout the war, escaped slaves, known as contrabands, had found their way to Union lines. There they were employed as cooks, waiters, teamsters, laborers, hospital attendants, and so on—just as in the South. But toward the end of the war, many had been armed.

After the Battle of Antietam, on September 17, 1862, when Lee was driven out of Maryland, Lincoln had announced his Emancipation Proclamation. He then made it official less than four months later, on January 1, 1863, when he declared all enslaved blacks in the Rebel states freed by his executive decree.

> "We've been to Vicksburg, Red River, Missouri, and about everywhere else . . . and now we're going to Hell."

Of course, that didn't free them, since he didn't yet control the Rebel states. But its practical effect was to allow Federal troops to free slaves as they advanced. As Lincoln had hoped, ex-slaves joined the Union forces in increasing numbers. Before the war was over, more than 186,000 blacks would fight for the North.

The use of ex-slaves as soldiers enraged the South, and the Confederate government refused to regard them, if captured, as normal prisoners of war. Instead, they threatened to kill them outright or re-enslave them. To discourage that, Lincoln issued an Executive Order on July 30, 1863, that threatened retaliation and appealed to international law:

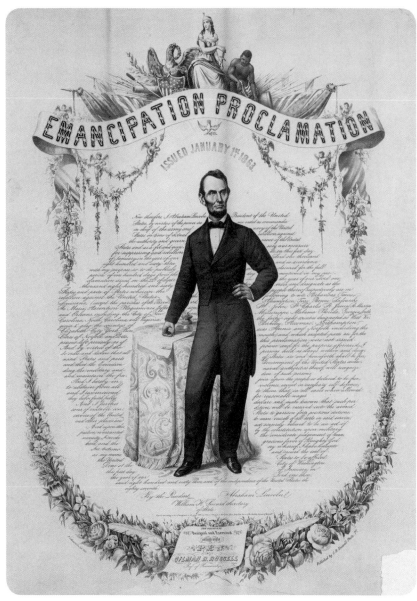

An artist's rendering of President Lincoln and the Emancipation Proclamation, published by Gilman R. Russell in 1863.

It is the duty of every Government to give protection to its citizens, of whatever class, color, or condition, and especially to those who are duly organized as soldiers in the public service. The law of nations and the usages and customs of war, as carried on by civilized powers, permit no distinction as to color in the treatment of prisoners of war as public enemies. To sell or enslave any captured person on account of his color, and for no offense against the laws of war, is a relapse into barbarism and a crime against the civilization of the age.

The Government of the United States will give the same protection to all its soldiers, and if the enemy shall sell or enslave anyone because of his color the offense shall be punished by retaliation upon the enemy's prisoners in our possession.

It is therefore ordered, *That for every soldier of the United States killed in violation of the laws of war a rebel soldier shall be executed, and for every one enslaved by the enemy or sold into slavery a rebel soldier shall be placed at*

*hard labor on the public works and continued at such labor
until the other shall be released and receive the treatment
due to a prisoner of war.*

Lincoln's historic proclamation was unwelcome to many
in the army. Some in the rank and file were opposed to it,
and some officers, too. Ulysses S. Grant, for one, was not
enthusiastic about arming blacks. And William Tecumseh
Sherman, who thought blacks inferior to whites, defied a
presidential order to brigade them with his men. He once
said, crudely: "A black man is good for stopping a bullet. But
a sandbag is better." Thomas, on the other hand, welcomed
blacks into his army and was devoted to their training and
care. Even though black soldiers had fought in a number of

*The charge of the third brigade at the
Battle of Nashville, sketched by
George H. Ellsbury in 1864.*

engagements before December 1864, it was Thomas alone who gave them their full dignity in battle and a major role in one of the decisive battles of the war.

That was one remarkable feature of his plan for the Nashville fight. Another was his use of cavalry. Throughout the war, both sides tended to send their cavalry on reconnaissance missions (to find out what the enemy was up to) or on raids to damage lines of communication and supply. They were good for such assignments because of their mobility and speed. But they had not been thought useful or effective as a combat unit on the regular battlefield. That meant that they were often absent from the scene of major battles where they might have tipped the scales. Hood made this mistake in early December, as he approached Nashville, when he sent cavalry commander Nathan Bedford Forrest off to try to capture a nearby town. At Nashville, however, Thomas planned to do something unique. He would use his cavalry as a key part of his attack. They would ride to their appointed places in the line of fire, dismount and fight as infantry, and then (if the enemy fled) remount for pursuit. He also armed them with seven-shot Spencer repeating carbines—so much more formidable than single-shot rifles— which gave them the firepower of a much stronger force.

Thomas placed his cavalry under the command of General James H. Wilson, the greatest of the "boy soldiers" of the war. Wilson had recently graduated from West Point but had shown so much intelligence, enterprise, and skill that Thomas saw at once that he was a man on whom he could rely. With his straight-backed military bearing, handsome face, slim figure, and elegant mustache, he was the very image of the dashing cavalry soldier.

On the morning of December 4, Hood's army, with flag fly-

General James Harrison Wilson, date unknown.

ing, drums beating, began to entrench opposite the Federal line. As if on holiday parade, his military bands began to play a number of popular tunes, including "Dixie"—a song of praise for the South—all along the line. Alexander Stewart's corps was on the left; S. D. Lee's in the center, astride the Franklin Turnpike; Cheatham's on the right. The cavalry, on the flanks, rested on the river above and below. Hood's line was four miles long, and five small forts, or redoubts, soon covered his flanks. He also had breastworks—temporary field fortifications such as earthworks thrown up to breast height for protection—to his front, and in one place the protection of a long stone wall. By his own count, he still had at least 45,000 left equipped with arms. Thomas had more, but only half were regular troops. His army was also not considered large enough to overrun strongly fortified positions. To do that, according to the usual thinking of the time, he would have needed two to three times as many troops as Hood.

Hood told his army chaplain he would win. He also predicted that there would be "more blood spilled in 1865 than in 1864—but . . . the losses will be on the Federal side." The whole war, he thought, was about to turn around. He had no intention of attacking Nashville itself, with its imposing fortifications, but he knew Thomas would be pressed to drive him away. He hoped to repulse him and, in a counterstroke, to take the town.

At Nashville, Thomas also had to be on his guard against the enemy within. Though Union troops had occupied the city since 1862, it remained a Rebel stronghold in spirit and swarmed with traitors, smugglers, and spies. Some of its menfolk were in the Confederate army, and their families passed on to them all the information they could. The city was like one vast "Southern Aid Society," as one Union of-

The war flag of General George H. Thomas, circa 1865–1880.

ficer put it. Thomas relied on a good-sized police force and an extensive secret service to keep things under control.

Meanwhile, Henry Halleck, Lincoln's army chief of staff; Edwin M. Stanton, his secretary of war; and General Grant had been sending Thomas nagging telegrams. As early as November 24, Grant (far away at City Point, Virginia) had begun to second-guess whatever Thomas did. On that day, he had wired Thomas not to "let Forrest get off without punishment." Thomas replied that he lacked the cavalry to do that because Sherman had taken all the good mounts. But "the moment I can get my cavalry, I will march against Hood, and if Forrest can be reached he shall be punished." Horses were requisitioned throughout Tennessee and Kentucky. Every possible mount, including those of a wandering circus, was rounded up. Not even Vice-President-Elect Andrew Johnson's fine stable of carriage horses was spared.

On December 1, Thomas wired Halleck that he needed a little more time, adding: "If Hood attacks me here, he will be more seriously damaged than he was [at Franklin]. If he remains until Wilson gets equipped, I can whip him."

Halleck ought to have been happy to hear it. Instead, he showed the telegram to Stanton, who talked to Lincoln about it. Stanton wired Grant that Lincoln was afraid Thomas might wait too long. Then Halleck wired Thomas: "If you wait till General Wilson mounts all his cavalry you will wait till doomsday." (General James H. Wilson, of course, was the fine young cavalry general Thomas had been counting on to execute an important part of his battle plan.)

Grant jumped at the idea that Thomas was too slow to act and began urging him to attack Hood at once. Thomas replied that he had "infantry enough" to do so, but still had more cavalry to mount. But he would "take the field anyhow" with what he had "in two or three days." That was unacceptable to Grant, who telegraphed Halleck on December 8: "If Thomas has not struck yet, he ought to be ordered to hand over his command to Schofield."

The authorities in Washington were dumbstruck. Lincoln may have wanted Grant to give Thomas a nudge, but he had not expected him to strip him of command.

Thomas would not be forced. He gave Wilson two more days to ready his mounts and wired Grant that he was convinced he had done everything as quickly as he could. The truth is, Sherman had left Thomas with a few thousand broken-down horses. In an amazingly short time, Thomas had assembled a first-rate cavalry force of 12,000 men. The wisdom of that would soon be plain. Even under pressure from Grant, Thomas was cool, quiet, careful in his movements, and, wrote one colleague, "a nice calculator of chances, intending to win all that could be won." Every day, in his opinion, increased the danger to Hood, while it improved the condition of the Union army. Why take desperate chances while a reasonable delay would render the outcome sure? Nothing was lost, much was gained.

As for Thomas's being slow, his delays were always tactical or strategic. "If he moved slowly," wrote one officer after the war, "he moved with irresistible power; and if he ground slowly, it was like the mills of the Gods."

Grant, however, had made up his mind. The next day (December 9), he carried through on his threat and wired Halleck: "Please telegraph orders relieving Thomas at once, and placing Schofield in command." Grant's order was prepared, but just as it was ready to be signed, an ice storm fell on the area about Nashville and froze both armies in place. The men could hardly get their footing, even on level ground. Halleck held on to the order throughout the day and told Grant of the change in weather that made it

A Union cavalryman in uniform, 1865.

*General John M. Schofield,
circa early 1860s.*

impossible for Thomas to act. He then asked Grant if he still wanted Thomas removed.

Grant became uneasy and drew back. Meanwhile, Thomas was indignant at the overall treatment he'd received. He called his fellow generals together and told them what was going on. All but Schofield (who sat sullen and silent) backed him up. When the conference came to an end, Thomas asked General James H. Wilson to stay behind. "Wilson," he said, "the Washington authorities treat me as if I were a boy. They seem to think me incapable of planning a campaign or of fighting a battle, but if they will just let me alone, I will show them what we can do."

The ice storm continued. No one was more impatient than Thomas for it to pass. He would sometimes sit by the window for an hour or more not speaking, gazing out upon the glazed hills. It was as if he were trying to will the storm away.

Then he heard again from Grant: "Delay no longer for weather or reinforcements." That was a mind-boggling order. How could Thomas launch an effective attack across ice-covered, open ground? It made no sense. Grant wasn't thinking clearly. Thomas replied (in a telegram to Halleck) that he thought an attack under such conditions "would only result in a useless sacrifice of life."

Meanwhile, General William Whipple, Thomas's chief of staff, thought there must be someone in their midst trying to bring Thomas down. Even Thomas, who had done everything correctly, and knew it, began to wonder, too. They were right. It later turned out that Schofield had been sending distorted information by wire to the War Department, which Halleck, Stanton, and Grant had picked up.

As if Thomas didn't have enough to deal with! He had a Judas on his staff!

Why would Schofield behave this way? One, he was an ally of Grant's. Two, as second in command, he stood to take over the army if Thomas was dismissed. Three, he had a grudge against Thomas that went back to his years at West Point. Thomas had been on the faculty then and had voted to expel Schofield for gross misconduct. But Schofield's sponsor (a United States senator) contrived to get him back in.

On December 13, Grant decided to go to Nashville himself to take charge. But the very next day, the ice storm stopped and a warm rain fell. Thomas drew a sigh of relief and his spirits rose. That afternoon, in a conference with his officers and aides, Thomas explained his final battle plan: by means of a carefully timed series of flank, frontal, and oblique attacks, Hood's forces would be caught and rolled up like a rug. First one wing of the Federal army would advance in such a way as to make Hood think the main attack was there. But it would be a feint and Hood would be deceived. However, he would shift his men to meet it. Then Thomas would launch his main attack at the other end of the field. Hood's line would be thrown back, and if all went well, his army would be crushed.

Thomas set his attack for dawn.

As dawn broke on December 15, a thick fog shrouded both camps. Thomas stood with his field glasses on a hill. From time to time, his head turned slowly as he surveyed the ground. Two hours passed. His staff, corps commanders, and thousands of men lay in ditches and rifle pits. The army had been in place since before daybreak. Their hearts pounded as they waited for the fog to lift. Thomas rode along the line to make sure everything was set. Shortly after eight the sun burned through and Thomas ordered the attack to begin. Up rose his men, with black troops in the forefront, and moved with terrific force against Hood's line.

They overran the Rebel breastworks and swarmed up the hills. On the left, right, and center, one after another, Hood's installations fell.

Then the greatest cavalry movement of the war began. Under the boyish Wilson, 12,000 mounted men made a wide detour around the Rebel left, dismounted, and advanced. Armed with the seven-shot Spencer repeating carbines, they cut their way through to the Confederate rear. Before long, the Rebels found themselves fighting on all sides.

Thousands of Nashville citizens watched the battle in horror from the rooftops and adjacent hills. "No army on the continent ever played on any field to so large and so sullen an audience," one Union officer wrote.

Evening fell just in time to save Hood's army from a rout. Even so, it had been forced back at all points with heavy losses. The Rebels retreated southward along every available road until they reached another outcropping of heights known as the Harpeth Hills. There Hood established a new line for the next day's fight.

As the casualty reports came in, it was clear that Hood had lost thousands of men, but Thomas relatively few. "So far I think we have done pretty well," Thomas remarked to an aide as he started back to Nashville to wire Grant of the day's success.

Grant was packing his suitcase at the Willard Hotel in Washington when he got the news. He was almost subdued. "I guess I will not go to Nashville," he said.

Early on December 16, Thomas rode along the line. His plan of attack for the second day was the same as the first. Once more, the infantry advanced to their front. Once more, the Federals attacked Hood's left obliquely as Wilson swung his cavalry by a wide detour to Hood's rear. A mixed brigade of black and white troops charged up a slope known

as Overton's Hill. The going was rough. Twice they were driven back. Yet on they came.

By mid-afternoon Wilson's dismounted cavalry had again gotten behind the Rebel army. Hood sent an urgent dispatch to his rear-guard cavalry commander: "For God's sake, drive the Yankee cavalry from our left and rear or all is lost."

It was then about half-past three. Thomas wheeled his

The army of General George H. Thomas at the Battle of Nashville. His troops are awaiting the order to attack.

right into place, poised to strike the final blow. A blast of artillery fire opened all along the line. Then the whole line advanced. One brigade after another swept the Rebels from their front. At the same time, Wilson's dismounted cavalry poured over the Rebel defenses in the rear.

All these movements were made in sequence, and "the whole Confederate left was crushed in like an egg-shell." Panic now seized the rest of Hood's army and spread like a virus through its ranks. Almost at once, that army broke and ran. Cheers of joy went up from the Federal ranks. That's "the voice of the American people," said Thomas as the cheers flowed back to where he stood. Black troops now surged up Overton's Hill, reached the summit, and chased the Confederates down the other side.

By the end of the afternoon, Hood's army had been utterly and completely destroyed. Five thousand men threw down their arms and surrendered in a single hour.

As the rest of the Rebels fled, the Federal cavalry, under the young and dashing Wilson, gave chase.

Thomas rode to the top of a hill, and, scanning the whole field of battle, he lifted his hat and cried, "Oh what a grand army I have! God bless each member of it." A little later, he came upon the bodies of black and white soldiers who had fallen together, mingled on the field. He was sick of bigoted talk in the army against the manhood of blacks. He turned to his staff and said, "Gentlemen, the issue is settled! Negroes will fight!" As the black regiments, who had played such a distinguished part in the triumph, marched out onto the Franklin Pike, Thomas turned his horse to the side of the road to face them and, with his head uncovered in a sign of respect, remained still until they had passed.

That night, as Wilson hurried his men in pursuit of Hood's army, he heard a horseman coming up at a gallop behind him. Suddenly Thomas himself loomed up in the darkness. He shouted out to him: "Is that you, Wilson? Dang it to hell, Wilson, didn't I tell you we could lick 'em, didn't I tell you?" With scarcely a pause for a reply, he wheeled his horse about. "Follow them as far as you can tonight," he cried, "and resume the pursuit as early as you can tomorrow morning," and at a gallop disappeared into the night.

The authorities in Washington abruptly changed their tune. The Northern press went wild with praise. GLORIOUS VICTORY AT NASHVILLE—HOOD'S ARMY COMPLETELY ROUTED, announced the *Chicago Tribune* in a headline. And the *New York Herald* proclaimed it THE HANDSOMEST VICTORY OF THE WAR.

In a battle that has since been called one of the two most perfectly planned and executed in military history—the other being Napoleon's victory at Austerlitz—Hood's army had been smashed as by a sledgehammer, and the cavalry that Thomas had carefully assembled over Grant's objections pursued its shattered remnants for ten days to make the victory complete. It was the one scientific battle of the war, and when it was over, Robert E. Lee and his army were all alone and the end was in sight. Four months later, Lee surrendered to Grant at Appomattox. But it was the Battle of Nashville that sealed his fate.

When word of Thomas's triumph first reached Washington, D.C., it came over the telegraph lines. The official in the War Department who received the wire at eleven that night ran down the stairs and hurried over to the house of Secretary of War Edwin Stanton. "What news?" asked Stanton from his second-story window. "Good news!" the man replied. Then he heard Stanton shout "Hurrah!" and his wife shout "Hurrah!" and their children (who ought to have been in bed) shout "Hurrah!" too. Stanton immediately rode to

The Battle of Nashville *by Louis Kurz and Alexander Allison, 1893.*

The surrender of General Robert E. Lee and his army to General Grant at Appomattox, artist unknown.

the White House himself to tell Lincoln. The president had retired for the night but was awakened. Soon he appeared in his nightshirt on the upstairs landing, holding a candle and looking like a ghost. But as Stanton began to speak, Lincoln's long, sad, wrinkled face broke into a huge smile. He knew what it meant. For the first time in a long time he looked almost happy—perhaps for the last time in his life.

POSTSCRIPT

After Lee surrendered, other Confederate forces in the South furled their flags. Meanwhile, early in April, in a campaign conceived, organized, and overseen by Thomas, three divisions of Federal cavalry under General James H. Wilson seized a number of Confederate strongholds. These included the important arsenals of Montgomery and Selma, Alabama. On May 10, in Georgia, Wilson's cavalry also captured Confederate president Jefferson Davis, who was disguised as an old woman in what appeared to be a bonnet and a dress.

For his victory at Nashville, Thomas was finally promoted to major general and in March received the thanks of Congress. After the war, he served as military governor of five Southern states and did as much as anyone could to make racial equality a reality under his rule. But as the general effort to reform the South (known as Reconstruction) faltered, he was the first to warn about the rise of a new, vicious organization known as the Ku Klux Klan. The Klan, in fact, was led by Nathan Bedford Forrest, the former Confederate commander and now a prominent citizen of the post-war South.

Meanwhile, Ulysses S. Grant had received a great deal of publicity after Lee's surrender and had become a political force to be reckoned with. With his constant cigar smoking and gambling, he cut a colorful figure for a time in the popular imagination. In 1868, he was elected president, due in part to this mystique. Toward the end of Grant's first term there was a widespread movement to draft Thomas for president and set him against Grant for the Republican nomination. But Thomas declined to get involved in politics. Many thought that had he been nominated, he could have taken the country by storm. In 1869, he was placed in charge of the army's Pacific command, with its headquarters in San Francisco. But his health had been broken by the war. On March 28, 1870, as he was writing a letter to a newspaper in response to a letter that slandered his career, a blood vessel burst in his brain.

His death was a national calamity.

With the single exception of George Washington, George H. Thomas was the greatest patriot-soldier America had ever produced.

His funeral was held on April 8, 1870, in Troy, New York. President Grant was there, as were many important political figures and generals, including William Tecumseh Sherman. The special train that had carried Thomas's body eastward from the Pacific just a few days before had been met by large, silent crowds at every station. Flags across the nation were flown at half-staff.

After a brief service, Thomas was buried in Oakwood Cemetery. At the special request of his widow, no eulogy was said over his grave.

In downtown Washington, D.C., today—at an intersection called Thomas Circle—there is a magnificent statue of General George H. Thomas on horseback. It was commissioned after his death by the men of his army and was cast in bronze from captured Confederate guns.

The unveiling of Thomas Circle in

Washington, D.C.

Lincoln's First Inaugural Address, March 4, 1861

[Full text]

Fellow-Citizens of the United States:

In compliance with a custom as old as the Government itself, I appear before you to address you briefly, and to take in your presence the oath prescribed by the Constitution of the United States to be taken by the President "before he enters on the execution of his office."

I do not consider it necessary at present for me to discuss those matters of administration about which there is no special anxiety or excitement.

Apprehension seems to exist among the people of the Southern States that by the accession of a Republican Administration their property and their peace and personal security are to be endangered. There has never been any reasonable cause for such apprehension. Indeed, the most ample evidence to the contrary has all the while existed and been open to their inspection. It is found in nearly all the published speeches of him who now addresses you. I do but quote from one of those speeches when I declare that "I have no purpose, directly or indirectly, to interfere with the institution of slavery in the States where it exists. I believe I have no lawful right to do so, and I have no inclination to do so." Those who nominated and elected me did so with full knowledge that I had made this and many similar declarations, and had never recanted them. And more than this, they placed in the platform for my acceptance, and as a law to themselves and to me, the clear and emphatic resolution which I now read:

"*Resolved,* That the maintenance inviolate of the rights of the States, and especially the right of each State to order and control its own domestic institutions, according to its own judgment exclusively, is essential to that balance of power on which the perfection and endurance of our political fabric depend, and we denounce the lawless invasion by armed force of the soil of any State or Territory, no matter what pretext, as among the gravest of crimes."

I now reiterate these sentiments; and, in doing so, I only press upon the public attention the most conclusive evidence of which the case is susceptible, that the property, peace, and security of no section are to be in any wise endangered by the now incoming Administration. I add, too, that all the protection which, consistently with the Constitution and the laws, can be given, will be cheerfully given to all the States when lawfully demanded, for whatever cause—as cheerfully to one section, as to another.

There is much controversy about the delivering up of fugitives from service or labor. The clause I now read is as plainly written in the Constitution as any other of its provisions:

"No person held to service or labor in one State, under the laws thereof, escaping into another, shall in consequence of any law or regulation therein be discharged from such service or labor, but shall be delivered up on claim of the party to whom such service or labor may be due."

It is scarcely questioned that this provision was intended by those who made it for the reclaiming of what we call fugitive slaves; and the intention of the lawgiver is the law.

All Members of Congress swear their support to the whole Constitution—to this provision as much as to any other. To the proposition, then, that slaves whose cases come within the terms of this clause, "shall be delivered up," their oaths are unanimous. Now, if they would make the effort in good temper, could they not with nearly equal unanimity frame and pass a law by means of which to keep good that unanimous oath?

There is some difference of opinion whether this clause should be enforced by national or by State authority, but surely that difference is not a very material one. If the slave is to be surrendered, it can be of but little consequence to him, or to others, by which authority it is done. And should any one, in any case, be content that his oath shall go unkept on a merely unsubstantial controversy as to *how* it shall be kept?

Again, in any law upon this subject, ought not all the safeguards of liberty known in civilized and humane jurisprudence to be introduced so that a free man be not, in any case, surrendered as a slave? And might it not be well at the same time to provide by law for the enforcement of that clause in the Constitution which guarantees that "the citizens of each State shall be entitled to all privileges and immunities of citizens in the several States"?

I take the official oath today with no mental reservations and with no purpose to construe the Constitution or laws by any hypercritical rules. And while I do not choose now to specify particular acts of Congress as proper to be enforced, I do suggest that it will be much safer for all, both in official and private stations, to conform to and abide by all those acts which stand unrepealed, than to violate any of them trusting to find impunity in having them held to be unconstitutional.

It is seventy-two years since the first inauguration of a President under our National Constitution. During that period fifteen different and greatly distinguished citizens have, in succession, administered the Executive branch of the Government. They have conducted it through many perils, and generally with great success. Yet, with all this scope of precedent, I now enter upon the same task for the brief constitutional term of four years under great and peculiar difficulty. A disruption of the Federal Union, heretofore only menaced, is now formidably attempted.

I hold that, in contemplation of universal law and of the Constitution, the Union of these States is perpetual. Perpetuity is implied, if not expressed, in the fundamental law of all national governments. It is safe to assert that no government proper ever had a provision in its organic law for its own termination. Continue to execute all the express provisions of our National Constitution, and the Union will endure forever—it being impossible to destroy it except by some action not provided for in the instrument itself.

Again, if the United States be not a Government proper, but an association of States in the nature of contract merely, can it, as a contract, be peaceably unmade by less than all the parties who made it? One party to a contract may violate it—break it, so to speak—but does it not require all to lawfully rescind it?

Descending from these general principles, we find the proposition that in legal contemplation, the Union is perpetual, confirmed by the history of the Union itself. The Union is much older than the Constitution. It was formed, in fact, by the Articles of Association in 1774. It was matured and continued by the Declaration of Independence in 1776. It was further matured, and the faith of all the then thirteen States expressly plighted and engaged that it should be perpetual, by the Articles of Confederation in 1778. And, finally, in 1787, one of the declared objects for ordaining and establishing the Constitution was, *"to form a more perfect Union."*

But if destruction of the Union by one, or by a part only, of the States be lawfully possible, the Union is less perfect than before the Constitution, having lost the vital element of perpetuity.

It follows from these views that no State, upon its own mere motion, can lawfully get out of the Union; that *resolves* and *ordinances* to that effect are legally void; and that acts of violence within any State or States, against the authority of the United States, are insurrectionary or revolutionary, according to circumstances.

I therefore consider that, in view of the Constitution and the laws, the Union is unbroken; and to the extent of my ability I shall take care, as the Constitution itself expressly enjoins upon me, that the laws of the Union be faithfully executed in all of the States. Doing this I deem to be only a simple duty on my part; and I shall perform it so far as practicable, unless my rightful masters, the American people, shall withhold the requisite means, or in some Authoritative manner direct the contrary. I trust this will not be regarded as a menace, but only as the declared purpose of the Union that it will constitutionally defend and maintain itself.

In doing this there needs to be no bloodshed or violence; and there shall be none, unless it be forced upon the national authority. The power confided to me will be used to hold, occupy, and possess the property and places belonging to the Government, and to collect the duties and imposts; but beyond what may be necessary for these objects, there will be no invasion, no using of force against or among the people anywhere. Where hostility to the United States, in any interior locality, shall be so great and universal as to prevent competent resident citizens from holding the Federal offices, there will be no attempt to force obnoxious strangers among the people for that object. While the strict legal right may exist in the Government to enforce the exercise of these offices, the attempt to do so would be so irritating, and so nearly impracticable withal, that I deem it better to forego for the time the uses of such offices.

The mails, unless repelled, will continue to be furnished in all parts of the Union. So far as possible, the people everywhere shall have that sense of perfect security which is most favorable to calm thought and reflection. The course here indicated will be followed unless current events and experience shall show a modification or change to be proper, and in every case and exigency my best discretion will be exercised according to circumstances actually existing, and with a view and a hope of a peaceful solution of the national troubles, and the restoration of fraternal sympathies and affections.

That there are persons in one section or another who seek to destroy the Union at all events, and are glad of any pretext to do it, I will neither affirm nor deny; but if there be such, I need address no word to them. To those, however, who really love the Union may I not speak?

Before entering upon so grave a matter as the destruction of our national fabric, with all its benefits, its memories, and its hopes, would it not be wise to ascertain precisely why we do it? Will you hazard so desperate a step while there is any possibility that any portion of the ills you fly from have no real existence? Will you, while the certain ills you fly to are greater than all the real ones you fly from — will you risk the commission of so fearful a mistake?

All profess to be content in the Union, if all constitutional rights can be maintained. Is it true, then, that any right, plainly written in the Constitution, has been denied? I think not. Happily, the human mind is so constituted, that no party can reach to the audacity of doing this. Think, if you can, of a single instance in which a plainly written provision of the Constitution has ever been denied. If by the mere force of numbers a majority should deprive a minority of any clearly written constitutional right, it might, in a moral point of view, justify revolution — certainly would if such a right were a vital one. But such is not our case. All the vital rights of minorities and of individuals are so plainly assured to them by affirmations and negations, guaranties and prohibitions, in the Constitution, that controversies never arise concerning them. But no organic law can ever be framed with a provision specifically applicable to every question which may occur in practical administration. No foresight can anticipate, nor any document of reasonable length contain, express provisions for all possible questions. Shall fugitives from labor be surrendered by national or by State authority? The Constitution does not expressly say. *May* Congress prohibit slavery in the Territories? The Constitution does not expressly say. *Must* Congress protect slavery in the Territories? The Constitution does not expressly say.

From questions of this class spring all our constitutional controversies, and we divide upon them into majorities and minorities. If the minority will not acquiesce, the majority must, or the Government must cease. There is no other alternative; for continuing the Government is acquiescence on one side or the other.

If a minority in such case will secede rather than acquiesce, they make a precedent which in turn will divide and ruin them; for a minority of their own will secede from them whenever a majority refuses to be controlled by such minority. For instance, why may not any portion of a new confederacy a year or two hence arbitrarily secede again, precisely as portions of the present Union now claim to secede from it? All who cherish disunion sentiments are now being educated to the exact temper of doing this.

Is there such perfect identity of interests among the States to compose a new Union as to produce harmony only, and prevent renewed secession?

Plainly, the central idea of secession is the essence of anarchy. A majority held in restraint by constitutional checks and limitations, and always changing easily with deliberate changes of popular opinions and sentiments, is the only true sovereign of a free people. Whoever rejects it does, of necessity, fly to anarchy or to despotism. Unanimity is impossible; the rule of a minority, as a permanent arrangement, is wholly inadmissible; so that, rejecting the majority principle, anarchy or despotism in some form is all that is left.

I do not forget the position, assumed by some, that constitutional questions are to be decided by the Supreme Court; nor do I deny that such decisions must be binding, in any case, upon the parties to a suit, as to the object of that suit, while they are also entitled to very high respect and consideration in all parallel cases by all other departments of the Government. And while it is obviously possible that such decision may be erroneous in any given case, still the evil effect following it, being limited to that particular case, with the chance that it may be overruled and never become a precedent for other cases, can better be borne than could the evils of a different practice. At the same time, the candid citizen must confess that if the policy of the Government, upon vital questions affecting the whole people, is to be irrevocably fixed by decisions of the Supreme Court, the instant they are made in ordinary litigation between parties in personal actions, the people will have ceased to be their own rulers, having to that extent practically resigned their Government into the hands of that eminent tribunal. Nor is there in this view any assault upon the court or the judges. It is a duty from which they may not shrink to decide cases properly brought before them, and it is no fault of theirs if others seek to turn their decisions to political purposes.

One section of our country believes slavery is *right,* and ought to be extended, while the other believes it is *wrong,* and ought not to be extended. This is the only substantial dispute. The fugitive-slave clause of the Constitution, and the law for the suppression of the foreign slave trade, are each as well enforced, perhaps, as any law can ever be in a community where the moral sense of the people imperfectly supports the law itself. The great body of the people abide by the dry legal obligation in both cases, and a few break over in each. This, I think, cannot be perfectly cured; and it would be worse in both cases *after* the separation of the sections than before. The foreign slave trade, now imperfectly suppressed, would be ultimately revived without restriction, in one section; while fugitive slaves, now only partially surrendered, would not be surrendered at all by the other.

Physically speaking, we cannot separate. We cannot remove our respective sections from each other, nor build an impassable wall between them. A husband and wife may be divorced, and go out of the presence and beyond the reach of each other; but the different parts of our country cannot do this. They cannot but remain face to face, and intercourse, either amicable or hostile, must continue between them. Is it possible, then, to make that intercourse more advantageous or more satisfactory *after* separation than *before*? Can aliens make treaties easier than friends can make laws? Can treaties be more faithfully enforced between aliens than laws can among friends? Suppose you go to war, you cannot fight always; and when, after much loss on both sides, and no gain on either, you cease fighting, the identical old questions as to terms of intercourse are again upon you.

This country, with its institutions, belongs to the people who inhabit it. Whenever they shall grow weary of the existing Government, they can exercise their *constitutional* right of amending it or their *revolutionary* right to dismember or overthrow it. I cannot be ignorant of the fact that many worthy and patriotic citizens are desirous of having the National Constitution amended. While I make no recommendation of amendments, I fully recognize the rightful authority of the people over the whole subject, to be exercised in either of the modes prescribed in the instrument itself; and I should, under existing circumstances, favor rather than oppose a fair opportunity being afforded the people to act upon it. I will venture to add that to me the convention mode seems preferable, in that it allows amendments to originate with the people themselves, instead of only permitting them to take or reject propositions originated by others, not especially chosen for the purpose, and which might not be precisely such as they would wish to either accept or refuse. I understand a proposed amendment to the Constitution—which amendment, however, I have not seen—has passed Congress, to the effect that the Federal Government shall never interfere with the domestic institutions of the States, including that of persons held to service. To avoid misconstruction of what I have said, I depart from my purpose, not to speak of particular amendments, so far as to say that, holding such a provision to now be implied constitutional law, I have no objection to its being made express and irrevocable.

The Chief Magistrate derives all his authority from the people, and they have conferred none upon him to fix terms for the separation of the States. The people themselves can do this also if they choose; but the Executive, as such, has nothing to do with it. His duty is to administer the present Government, as it came to his hands, and to transmit it, unimpaired by him, to his successor.

Why should there not be a patient confidence in the ultimate justice of the people? Is there any better or equal hope in the world? In our present differences, is either party without faith of being in the right? If the Almighty Ruler of Nations, with His eternal truth and justice, be on your side of the North, or on yours of the South, that truth and that justice will surely prevail by the judgment of this great tribunal of the American people.

By the frame of the Government under which we live, this same people have wisely given their public servants but little power for mischief; and have, with equal wisdom, provided for the return of that little to their own hands at very short intervals. While the people retain their virtue and vigilance, no Administration, by any extreme of wickedness or folly, can very seriously injure the Government in the short space of four years.

My countrymen, one and all, think calmly and well upon this whole subject. Nothing valuable can be lost by taking time. If there be an object to *hurry* any of you in hot haste to a step which you would never take *deliberately*, that object will be frustrated by taking time; but no good object can be frustrated by it. Such of you as are now dissatisfied still have the old Constitution unimpaired, and, on the sensitive point, the laws of your own framing under it; while the new Administration will have no immediate power, if it would, to change either. If it were admitted that you who are dissatisfied hold the right side in the dispute, there still

rend the Union even by war, while the Government claimed no right to do more than to restrict the territorial enlargement of it. Neither party expected for the war the magnitude or the duration which it has already attained. Neither anticipated that the *cause* of the conflict might cease with or even before the conflict itself should cease. Each looked for an easier triumph, and a result less fundamental and astounding. Both read the same Bible and pray to the same God, and each invokes His aid against the other. It may seem strange that any men should dare to ask a just God's assistance in wringing their bread from the sweat of other men's faces, but let us judge not, that we be not judged. The prayers of both could not be answered. That of neither has been answered fully. The Almighty has His own purposes. "Woe unto the world because of offenses; for it must needs be that offenses come, but woe to that man by whom the offense cometh." If we shall suppose that American slavery is one of those offenses which, in the providence of God, must needs come, but which, having continued through His appointed time, He now wills to remove, and that He gives to both North and South this terrible war as the woe due to those by whom the offense came, shall we discern therein any departure from those divine attributes which the believers in a living God always ascribe to Him? Fondly do we hope, fervently do we pray, that this mighty scourge of war may speedily pass away. Yet, if God wills that it continue until all the wealth piled by the bondsman's two hundred and fifty years of unrequited toil shall be sunk, and until every drop of blood drawn with the lash shall be paid by another drawn with the sword, as was said three thousand years ago, so still it must be said "the judgments of the Lord are true and righteous altogether."

With malice toward none, with charity for all, with firmness in the fight as God gives us to see the right, let us strive on to finish the work we are in, to bind up the nation's wounds, to care for him who shall have borne the battle and for his widow and his orphan, to do all which may achieve and cherish a just and lasting peace among ourselves and with all nations.

Selections from the Thirteenth, Fourteenth, & Fifteenth Amendments to the CONSTITUTION of the UNITED STATES

These amendments were adopted after the Civil War to ensure full citizenship rights for all. The relevant sections are given below.

Amendment 13 (ratified December 6, 1865)

Section 1. Neither slavery nor involuntary servitude, except as a punishment for crime whereof the party shall have been duly convicted, shall exist within the United States, or any place subject to their jurisdiction.

Amendment 14 (ratified July 9, 1868)

Section 1. All persons born or naturalized in the United States, and subject to the jurisdiction thereof, are citizens of the United States and of the State wherein they reside. No State shall make or enforce any law which shall abridge the privileges or immunities of citizens of the United States; nor shall any State deprive any person of life, liberty, or property, without due process of law; nor deny to any person within its jurisdiction the equal protection of the laws.

Amendment 15 (ratified February 3, 1870)

Section 1. The right of citizens of the United States to vote shall not be denied or abridged by the United States or by any State on account of race, color, or previous condition of servitude.

Notes

Chapter One

"I had a physique": James Grant Wilson, *Ulysses S. Grant*, p. 101.

"Tell me the brand": Wilbur F. Gordy, *Abraham Lincoln*, p. 224.

"scraped clean": Isaac Thomas, ed., *The Words of Abraham Lincoln*, p. 22.

"That coffee smells good": Gordy, *Abraham Lincoln*, p. 212.

"Die when I may": ibid., p. 211.

"man and beast were one": William O. Stoddard, *Ulysses S. Grant*, p. 24.

Anecdote about Grant's plug hat: Lavern M. Hamand, "Coles County in the Civil War," *Eastern Illinois University Bulletin*, no. 234, p. 60.

"I just thought I would jump": Jean Edward Smith, *Grant*, p. 376.

"He looked like an undertaker": ibid.

Chapter Two

"We hold these truths": James Brown Scott, ed., *Founding Documents*, p. 3.

"three-fifths": ibid., p. 29.

"There is really no Union now": John Sherman, *John Sherman's Recollections of Forty Years in the U.S. Senate, House, and Cabinet*, vol. 1, p. 100.

"A house divided against itself": Thomas, *The Words of Abraham Lincoln*, pp. 27–28.

"Friends, this thing has been delayed": Gordy, *Abraham Lincoln*, p. 96.

"All we ask": W. R. Brock, ed., *The Civil War*, p. 7.

"These all against us": James Lee McDonough, *War in Kentucky*, p. 61.

"In *your* hands, my dissatisfied fellow-countrymen": Lincoln's First Inaugural Address.

Chapter Three

"My paramount object": Thomas, *The Words of Abraham Lincoln*, pp. 169–70.

"I had been fishing": Gordy, *Abraham Lincoln*, p. 5.

Chapter Four

"Whichever way he turned the matter over": Henry Coppée, *General Thomas*, p. 36.

"He loved the Negro quarters": James Grant Wilson and Titus Munson Coan, eds., *Personal Recollections of the War of the Rebellion*, p. 287.

"against his parents' orders": ibid.

"crossroad villages": Stephen B. Oates, *The Fires of Jubilee*, p. 2.

"a smoky cluster": ibid., p. 1.

"drops of dew": F. Roy Johnson, *The Nat Turner Slave Insurrection*, p. 231.

"leaves with strange": ibid., p. 234.

"For as the blood of Christ": ibid.

"like a black hand": Oates, *The Fires of Jubilee*, p. 55.

"Alone with the fox's bark": Eric Foner, *Nat Turner*, p. 135.

"Mr. Lincoln, in the early part of the war": Coppée, *General Thomas*, pp. 319–20.

Chapter Five

"I will hold McClellan's horse": Gordy, *Abraham Lincoln*, p. 168.

"I know that a few thousand more men": ibid., p. 171.

"If we gave McClellan": ibid.

"The Yankees are coming!": John Fitch, *Annals of the Army*

of the Cumberland, p. 631.

"I can't spare this man": Alexander K. McClure, *Lincoln and Men of War-Times*, p. 196.

"like putting one's hand in a sack": Donn Piatt and Henry V. Boynton, *General George H. Thomas: A Critical Biography*, p. 268.

Chapter Six

"We don't have more than half": Benson Bobrick, *Testament: A Soldier's Story of the Civil War*, p. 39.

"There are new cases": ibid., p. 47.

"It is redicklous": William L. Shea and Earl L. Hess, *Pea Ridge: Civil War Campaign in the West*, p. 253.

"I don't believe he could have suffered": ibid.

"Oh Mother; How can I say it!": Bobrick, *Testament*, p. 110.

"I would rather go": ibid., p. 216.

"The boys are in their tents": ibid.

"Who are you?": Fitch, *Annals of the Army of the Cumberland*, p. 653.

"You're a Yankee, right?": ibid., p. 675.

"Next to the Army of the Potomac": Wilbur Thomas, *General George H. Thomas: The Indomitable Warrior*, p. 27.

Chapter Seven

"None of us": Gordy, *Abraham Lincoln*, p. 195.

"Hello, comrade": ibid., p. 198.

"My God!, My God!": ibid., p. 196.

"The Father of Waters": Piatt and Boynton, *General George H. Thomas*, p. 375.

"Four score and seven years ago": *Abraham Lincoln*, Gettysburg Address.

"like a team of balky horses": Ronald H. Bailey, *Battles for Atlanta: Sherman Moves East*, p. 20.

"one big Indian fight": ibid., p. 75.

Chapter Eight

"The art of war is simple enough": James I. Robertson, Jr.,
  The Civil War, p. 54.
"If there was a cheerful face present": Military Order of the
  Loyal Legion of the United States, Indiana Commandery,
  War Papers, vol. 1, p. 174.
"Gentlemen, this army can't retreat!": Coppée, *General
  Thomas*, pp. 100–101.
"Hold Chattanooga": Thomas B. Van Horne, *The Life of Major
  General George H. Thomas*, p. 156.
"We will hold": ibid.
"jealous": Gideon Welles, *The Diary of Gideon Welles*, vol. 2,
  pp. 282–83.

Chapter Nine

"ready to risk all": Coppée, *General Thomas*, pp. 238–39.
"I know what hole": Don E. and Virginia Fehrenbacher, eds.,
  Recollected Words of Abraham Lincoln, p. 403.
"a slaughter pen": *Tennessee Historical Quarterly*, vol. 64, no. 3,
  p. 190.
"his hat lifted": James F. Rusling, *Men and Things I Saw in Civil
  War Days*, p. 86.
"We're A. J. Smith's guerrillas": ibid.
"It is the duty of every Government": Roy P. Basler, ed.,
  The Collected Works of Abraham Lincoln, vol. 6, p. 357.
"A black man is good": Anne J. Bailey, *The Chessboard of War:
  Sherman and Hood in the Autumn Campaigns of 1864*, p. 231.
"more blood spilled": Richard M. McMurry, *John Bell Hood*,
  p. 178.
"Southern Aid Society": Fitch, *Annals of the Army of the
  Cumberland*, p. 373.
"let Forrest get off": Piatt and Boynton, *General George H.
  Thomas*, p. 652.
"the moment I can get": Van Horne, *The Life of Major General
  George H. Thomas*, p. 300.
"If Hood attacks me": ibid.

"If you wait till": Richard W. Johnson, *Memoir of Major-General George H. Thomas*, p. 188.

"infantry enough": *War of the Rebellion: A Compilation of the Official Records of the Union and Confederate Armies*, 1st series, vol. 45, Part 2, p. 18.

"If Thomas has not struck yet": Wilson, *Under the Old Flag*, vol. 2, p. 96.

"a nice calculator of chances": Coppée, *General Thomas*, p. 265.

"If he moved slowly": Ell Torrance, "General George H. Thomas," p. 20.

"Please telegraph orders": *War of the Rebellion: Official Records*, 1st series, vol. 45, Part 2, p. 97.

"Wilson, the Washington authorities": Wilson, *Under the Old Flag*, vol. 2, p. 102.

"Delay no longer for weather or reinforcements": *War of the Rebellion: Official Records*, 1st series, vol. 45, Part 2, p. 155.

"would only result": ibid.

"No army on the continent": Mark Zimmermann, *Guide to Civil War Nashville*, p. 52.

"So far I think": Rusling, *Men and Things I Saw in Civil War Days*, p. 96.

"I guess I will not": Wilson, *Under the Old Flag*, vol. 2, p. 95.

"For God's sake": *Tennessee Historical Quarterly*, vol. 64, no. 3, p. 258.

"the whole Confederate left": Matthew Forney Steele, *American Campaigns*, vol. 1, p. 576.

"the voice of the American people": Rusling, *Men and Things I Saw in Civil War Days*, p. 101.

"Oh what a grand army I have!": Johnson, *Memoir of Major-General George H. Thomas*, p. 195.

"Gentlemen, the issue is settled!": Noah Andre Trudeau, *Like Men of War: Black Troops in the Civil War, 1862–1865*, p. 349, fn. 32.

"Is that you, Wilson?": Wilson, *Under the Old Flag*, vol. 2, p. 126.

"What news?": David Homer Bates, *Lincoln in the Telegraph Office: Recollections of the United States Military Telegraph Corps During the Civil War*, p. 317.

Some Books About the Civil War

Bailey, Anne J. *The Chessboard of War: Sherman and Hood in the Autumn Campaigns of 1864.* Lincoln: University of Nebraska Press, 2000.

Bailey, Ronald H. *Battles for Atlanta: Sherman Moves East.* New York: Time-Life Books, 1985.

Basler, Roy P., ed. *The Collected Works of Abraham Lincoln.* 9 vols. New Brunswick, N.J.: Rutgers University Press, 1953–55.

Bates, David Homer. *Lincoln in the Telegraph Office: Recollections of the United States Military Telegraph Corps During the Civil War.* New York: Century, 1907.

Bobrick, Benson. *Master of War: The Life of General George H. Thomas.* New York: Simon & Schuster, 2009.

———. *Testament: A Soldier's Story of the Civil War.* New York: Simon & Schuster, 2003.

Brock, W. R., ed. *The Civil War.* New York: Harper & Row, 1969.

Buell, Thomas B. *The Warrior Generals: Combat Leadership in the Civil War.* New York: Crown, 1997.

Castel, Albert. *Winning and Losing in the Civil War: Essays and Stories.* Columbia: University of South Carolina Press, 1996.

Catton, Bruce. Edited by James M. McPherson. *American Heritage New History of the Civil War.* New York: Viking, 1996.

———. *The Civil War.* New York: American Heritage, 1960.

Cist, Henry M. *Army of the Cumberland: Campaigns of the Civil War.* New York: Scribner, 1892.

Coppée, Henry. *General Thomas.* New York: Appleton, 1893.

Dwight, Theodore F., ed. *Critical Sketches of Some of the Federal and Confederate Commanders.* Boston: Houghton Mifflin, 1895.

Fehrenbacher, Don E. and Virginia, eds. *Recollected Words of Abraham Lincoln.* Palo Alto, Calif.: Stanford University Press, 1996.

Fiske, John. *The Mississippi Valley in the Civil War.* Boston: Houghton Mifflin, 1900.

Fitch, John. *Annals of the Army of the Cumberland.* Philadelphia: Lippincott, 1864.

Foner, Eric. *Nat Turner.* Englewood Cliffs, N.J.: Prentice Hall, 1971.

Foote, Shelby. *The Civil War.* 3 vols. New York: Vintage, 1986.

Freedman, Russell. *Lincoln: A Photobiography.* New York: Clarion, 1987.

Gordy, Wilbur F. *Abraham Lincoln.* New York: Scribner, 1917.

Grant, Ulysses S. *Personal Memoirs.* New York: Penguin Classics, 1999.

Hamand, Lavern M. "Coles County in the Civil War," *Eastern Illinois University Bulletin*, no. 234, April 1961.

Horn, Stanley F. The Decisive Battle of Nashville. Baton Rouge: Louisiana State University Press, 1984.

Johnson, F. Roy. *The Nat Turner Slave Insurrection.* Murfreesboro, N.C.: Johnson, 1966.

Johnson, Richard W. *Memoir of Major-General George H. Thomas.* Philadelphia: Lippincott, 1881.

McClure, Alexander K. *Lincoln and Men of War-Times.* Philadelphia: Times Publishing, 1892.

McDonough, James Lee. *War in Kentucky.* Knoxville: University of Tennessee Press, 1994.

McMurry, Richard M. *John Bell Hood.* Lexington: University of Kentucky Press, 1982.

Military Order of the Loyal Legion of the United States, Indiana Commandery. *War Papers*, vol. 1. Wilmington, N.C.: Broadfoot, 1994.

Monaghan, Jay. *Civil War on the Western Border, 1854–1865.* New York: Bonanza, 1955.

Oates, Stephen B. *The Fires of Jubilee: Nat Turner's Fierce Rebellion.* New York: Harper & Row, 1975.

Piatt, Donn, and Henry V. Boynton. *General George H. Thomas: A Critical Biography.* Cincinnati: Robert Clarke, 1893.

Robertson, James I., Jr. *The Civil War.* Washington, D.C.: U.S. Civil War Centennial Commission, 1963.

Rusling, James F. *Men and Things I Saw in Civil War Days.* New York: Eaton & Mains, 1899.

Scott, James Brown, ed. *Founding Documents.* New York: Oxford University Press, 1917.

Shea, William L., and Earl L. Hess. *Pea Ridge: Civil War Campaign in the West.* Chapel Hill: University of North Carolina Press, 1997.

Sherman, John. *John Sherman's Recollections of Forty Years in the U.S. Senate, House, and Cabinet.* 2 vols. Chicago: Werner, 1895.

Sherman, William Tecumseh. *Memoirs.* New York: Penguin Classics, 2000.

Smith, Jean Edward. *Grant.* New York: Simon & Schuster, 2002.

Steele, Matthew Forney. *American Campaigns.* 2 vols. Washington, D.C.: U.S. Infantry Association, 1931.

Stoddard, William O. *Ulysses S. Grant.* New York: Frederick A. Stokes, 1886.

Tennessee Historical Quarterly, vol. 64, no. 3 (fall 2005).

Thomas, Isaac, ed. *The Words of Abraham Lincoln.* Chicago: Western Publishing House, 1898.

Thomas, Wilbur. *General George H. Thomas: The Indomitable Warrior.* New York: Expository, 1964.

Torrance, Ell. "General George H. Thomas." Pamphlet, Address to the Minnesota Commandery of the Military Order of the Loyal Legion of the United States, March 9, 1897.

Trudeau, Noah Andre. *Like Men of War: Black Troops in the Civil War, 1862–1865.* Boston: Little, Brown, 1998.

Van Horne, Thomas B. *The Life of Major General George H. Thomas.* New York: Scribner, 1882.

The War of the Rebellion: A Compilation of the Official Records of the

Union and Confederate Armies. 128 vols. Washington, D.C.: U.S. Government Printing Office, 1880–1901.

Welles, Gideon. *The Diary of Gideon Welles.* 3 vols. Boston: Houghton Mifflin, 1911.

Wilson, James Grant. *Ulysses S. Grant.* New York: Appleton, 1897.

Wilson, James Grant, and Titus Munson Coan, eds. *Personal Recollections of the War of the Rebellion.* New York: New York Commandery of the Military Order of the Loyal Legion of the United States, 1891.

Wilson, James H. *Under the Old Flag.* 2 vols. New York: Appleton, 1912.

Zimmermann, Mark. *Guide to Civil War Nashville.* Nashville: Battle of Nashville Preservation Society, 2004.

PICTURE CREDITS

All images courtesy of Library of Congress Prints and Photographs Division, special exhibition American Treasures of the Library of Congress, and American Memory from the Library of Congress except:

The Battle of Nashville by Howard Pyle, pp. 84–85 Credit: © Minnesota Historical Society/CORBIS

Battle of Nashville Preservation Society, Inc.: p. 82. Used with the permission of the Battle of Nashville Preservation Society, Inc.

Bob Redman/www.aotc.net, © Aug. 11, 2003: p. 34

Bob Redman/www.aotc.net: p. 35

National Archives and Records Administration: pp. 64, 74

Shutterstock.com: pp. ii–iii, 133

Special thanks to the creators of www.sonofthesouth.net for all their help.

INDEX

Page references in *italics* refer to illustrations.